Wake up...
Live the Life You Love,

A Power Within

Little Seed Publishing, LLC
P.O. Box 4483
Laguna Beach, CA 92652

Pre-Press Management by New Caledonian Press

Text and Cover Design: Wm. Gross Magee

Acknowledgement is made for permission to quote copyrighted materials.

Printed in the United States of America

Distributed by Global Partnership, LLC
608-B Main Street
Murray, KY 42071

Library of Congress Cataloguing-In-Publication Data
ISBN: 1-933063-04-1

$14.95 USA $20.45 Canada

Other books by Steven E and Lee Beard

Wake Up...Live the Life You Love

Wake Up...Live the Life You Love, Second Edition

Wake Up...Shape Up...Live the Life You Love

Wake Up...Live the Life You Love, Inspirational How-to Stories

Wake Up...Live the Life You Love, In Beauty

Wake Up...Live the Life You Love, Living on Purpose

Wake Up...Live the Life You Love, Finding Your Life's Passion

Wake Up...Live the Life You Love, Purpose, Passion, Abundance

Wake Up...Live the Life You Love, Finding Personal Freedom

Wake Up...Live the Life You Love, Seizing Your Success

Wake Up...Live the Life You Love, Giving Gratitude

Wake Up...Live the Life You Love, On the Enlightened Path

Wake Up...Live the Life You Love, In Spirit

For your free gift, go to: **www.wakeupand.com**

How would you like to be in the next book
with a fabulous group of best-selling authors?
Another Wake Up book is coming soon!

Visit: WakeUpLive.com

We would like to provide you with a free gift
to enhance this book experience. For your
free gift, please visit: WakeUpGift.com

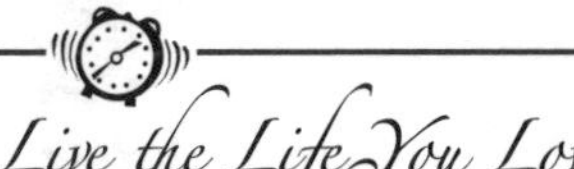

Contents

Goals Are Damaging

John Di Lemme

Can you relate to setting goals and not achieving them? Have you ever been frustrated over trying to set goals when you've known in your heart that you would never reach them? You might say to yourself, "Who am I kidding? I will never accomplish this goal." That's why I'm telling you that goals can be truly damaging for your future. You may beat yourself up because you never reach those goals. Eventually you just give up.

On the other hand, goals are very important. Goals are imperative when you have a strong *Why* in place. Let's compare your goals to a ten-story glass building, shiny and beautiful to the eye. It towers over the city and enhances the skyline. Now let's imagine that the building had been built by a group of amateur carpenters in one day and it had a poor foundation. It looked very nice, but it wasn't solid. One day a tiny sparrow smacks into that building. Guess what happens? That little bird knocks down that apparently strong and powerful-looking building. Why? There were no true roots holding it in place. No one had paid the price for that building to hold its own in the real world. It had no foundation to sustain and support it.

Now, let's tie that analogy to your goals. Your *Why* is your foundation and your roots. What is a *Why*? It is simply your purpose for living and your ultimate goal in life. Your *Why* must be stronger and bigger than you are. You must internalize your *Why* and know exactly *Why* you do what you do everyday to reach your goals. Too many people have set a goal to make a lot of money. Many find that they set a goal to make a certain amount of money in a month, and then, at the end of the month, they haven't made a dime more. You must know *why* you want to earn that amount of money for that month. It's not the money that drives you—it's your *Why*!

What were you going to do with the money? Make your car payment? Donate it to your church? Buy your child a new toy? You should never set a goal of "making" a certain amount of money in a given time. Instead, first decide *why* you are setting the financial goal and then, set a goal of earning the money. Remember: the

building fell because the builder's weren't willing to work hard enough to make it sturdy. You must be willing to pay the price and earn your goal.

Remember, setting goals can be damaging. If you don't have your *Why* in place, then you have no foundation to support you as you set out to achieve your goals. You will give up and be discouraged.

Here are three questions that will help you find your *Why*;

1. If you did not have to worry about your finances; if you didn't have to work on Monday morning, what would you do?
2. Suppose you had so much money that you had to give it away. Who would you give it to and why?
3. Do you enjoy life? Why? Why not? Remember, your past does not control you! Your future should drive you because you see yourself as a success.

After you develop your *Why* and set your goals, you will inevitably encounter obstacles and challenges. If your *Why* is strong enough though, you can stand firm. You will not be knocked down!

I challenge you today to ask yourself those three questions, develop your *Why*, and set your goals. Your *Why* will become a new force in your life and your future will beckon you as never before.

ᔕ John Di Lemme

Freedom

Stephen Rogers

In the eighties, I stepped into a culture of violence, drug and steroid abuse, body building and alcoholism, while I established myself as a mid-level drug dealer. Contrary to the stereotype of drug dealers, I wasn't in it for the money or power, though those things were nice. I got into the drug business for the pseudo sense of freedom it gave me. In fact, it was nothing more than self-avoidance hidden by child-like rebellion.

Finally the day came and there I was, broken to pieces. It was 2:00 A.M. and I was all alone, a thousand miles from home in a hill-billy motel room. I awoke from a dream in which the police arrested me. Whoa! I freaked, considering I was waiting for business. The dream flung me over a paranoid edge. So, I began to pray. Yes, I got down on my hands and knees and made the most honest, humble commitment of my entire life. It went something like this, "God, Jesus, Buddha, Allah, Great White Energy, or whatever you are, I want to be FREE! I will do anything you need me to do to be free!" (FYI: If you ever decide to get serious about being free and tell God that you will do *anything,* remember this; God can't take a joke.)

Shortly after reflecting, I fell asleep. The next morning as I was walking my dog, two cars came speeding toward me from different ends of the motel parking lot. At first I thought they were dope robbers, guys who rob dealers, which was common in the area. I thought, "Oh man, I'm going to get shot-n-killed by these hill jacks a thousand miles from home and no one is going to know." A guy jumped from one car and put a gun to my face. With his other hand, in what seemed like slow motion, he pulled out an FBI badge. "Amen! It's the cops," I thought as my bladder emptied.

Living hell began then. It turned out that several law enforcement agencies had a huge amount of evidence piled against me, and I was looking at some lengthy sentences. I made the choice to become a confidential informant for the FBI in return for less prison time. My life spiraled chaotically as I continued to rely on drugs to calm the stress. The constant deception of being a snitch overwhelmed me. This went on for one drawn-out year. By the end of that year, I had gained 50 pounds, lost my fiancée, lost my home and developed a crack addiction. I lived in my car and slept on friends' couches. Finally, I landed in prison to serve an 18 month federal sentence. When I arrived, I was in awful shape, but relieved to be out of the chaos of the drug culture.

After processing, I awoke in solitary, the hole. The realization of my situation hit me like a ton of bricks. Federal prison was my new home and 550 snitch-hating convicts were my new roommates. What a dilemma: I was stuck in a nine-by-six box with nowhere to go. No television, no sugar, no drugs, no alcohol, no sex, no caffeine, and no one to talk to. Yet, that wasn't the worst of it. There I was, and there was a familiar suffocating pain in my chest. It felt incapacitating, and I had nothing to take the edge off.

For the remaining 48 hours in the hole, it felt like I came apart. I understand it now, but then I just held on blindly for dear life. My body and mind went through a metamorphosis or mind-body transformation. My hands, feet, head, and heart burned painfully with electric-like heat. My spine wrenched, unraveled, and lengthened in all directions involuntarily. I thought I was losing my mind. These symptoms continued for months, until one night, I finally felt relief. An incredible surge of energy moved from my heart to my head, leaving a peace and brightness beyond words. Of course, that was just the beginning of the mind-body transformation. The innate process of melting my heart continues to evolve even to this day.

While I was in prison, something became very clear to me. Most everyone suffers from the imprisoned condition of a closed heart. In order to be free of this condition, we all must ask ourselves three questions: "Do I want to be free?" "Do I want to be free more than anything else?" "What am I willing to do to be free?" After we ask these questions with brutal honesty, then we can truly know what motivates our intention for freedom and whether or not we authentically want to be free. If we truly desire freedom, life will direct us to it, like a river bursting through a dam to reach the valley's floor. Nothing can stop freedom.

If you are not rooted and grounded in freedom, then ask yourself the above questions. After much reflection, in time, your answers will come. Remember, when I got down on my hands and knees asking for freedom, I committed, "I'll do anything." Are you ready to do anything? Do you want to be free?

Stephen Rogers

Love, Friendship, and the Miracle of a Carol King Concert

Kathy Kunau

As a student of "A Course in Miracles," I had been asking Jesus to reveal God's plan for my life when I began hearing what I call "the voice for God." Most of the time, I didn't understand the reasons for the guidance I was receiving. However, I found time and again that it would become clear to me somewhere along the way and I would be so grateful. My life was becoming one of constant amazement with the synchronicities and miracles that happened when I followed the voice. This is the story of one of those miracles.

I was in a hotel bar sitting next to two women who had just returned from a very fun vacation in Mexico. We started talking. The conversation changed. I realized that one of the women, I'll call her Mary, had had a particularly difficult divorce and was still in pain. As I listened to her, I heard the voice say, "Holographic Repatterning." I briefly told her about it and gave her a brochure. I gently let her know that this amazing process had helped me to remove the pain I had experienced after my break-up a few months earlier. More importantly, it had helped me to remove the blocks to what I wanted most in my life, receiving God's guidance clearly. I assumed God wanted Mary to know about Holographic Repatterning because it would help her too. We traded phone numbers and talked about possibly walking together sometime.

A couple of days later, the voice guided me to call Mary and ask whether I could join her when she went walking. Initially, I was reluctant to call. I wasn't in the best shape and Mary, who was much more fit than I, said that they typically walked anywhere from five to ten miles. I had no idea how I would be able to keep up. But, that voice of God that was my guidance told me go.

That walk began a ritual that we kept several times a week throughout the rest of the summer. Within days of my first walk with Mary, the voice told me that Mary felt hopeless and my job was to listen to the voice and give Mary the messages I was hearing. This seemed a bit extreme to me, given what I knew about Mary at that point. However, something in me knew that the guide I was hearing knew far more than I.

A few days later, Mary told me that she didn't want to live anymore and that she had felt that way for some time. I knew I had to follow the voice. The messages were simple and I was just the messenger. The primary message was that God loved her, and of the importance of forgiveness. I knew how difficult it could be to forgive. I also knew from my own experience that love and forgiveness were the only way out of the hell she was in. Mary hadn't forgiven her ex-husband, and that was what she needed to do before she could live, love, and enjoy life again.

Mary would talk and I would listen to the voice. I let God speak through me. I began confiding that I was hearing the voice and conveying the messages as I understood them. She listened and, surprisingly, didn't laugh. We were learning together and helping each other. I began to realize that this was the purpose of this and every relationship.

One morning, the voice guided me to buy tickets to a Carol King concert. I thought I should at least make sure Mary wanted to go before I bought the tickets. They weren't exactly cheap, and I wasn't in the habit of doing such extravagant things out of the blue like that. But the guidance was clear: "Just get the tickets." I bought the tickets.

That night when we met, I asked Mary if she liked Carol King. I don't know why I was surprised to hear, "Do I like Carol King? Oh my God, I still have the vinyl! Carol King's one of my all time favorites!" She went on about how she knew all her songs by heart and played her at every party she had ever had. This was her reaction before I told her she was going to the concert. Words can't begin to describe the look on her face when I said, "Well, you're going to the Carol King concert." Mary told me that just days earlier she had seen the ad for the concert and "wished to God that she could go." During the concert, I witnessed the joy Mary received and thanked God for this wonderful miracle.

Mary gave me a gift box with a number of little individually wrapped gifts, each with a hand-written note attached. The box contained a wide range of items that represented my life. Mary wanted me to know that she had been listening too. I was touched beyond belief. Some were fun and silly; others just very thoughtful. The one that brought tears was a bookmark with a Gandhi quote: "Where There Is Love, There Is Life." And her note said, "Here's a reminder of what you gave me."

Mary needed to know–with maybe a little proof–that first and foremost God loved her. I was lucky that He used me to deliver this message. It's truly amazing what happens when we just listen to each other and God. God is in all of us and everyone we meet has a message.

I thank God for the miracle of my new friend Mary, a Carol King concert, and all that Mary has given me. It is now and forever a part of me.

Kathy Kunau

Victim or Victor

Betty Anderson

I was raised on a farm, blessed by having two loving, God-fearing parents. They believed in honesty, integrity, hard work, and me. My wonderful parents had visions of me attending university and becoming a doctor, lawyer, or business graduate and having a career of prestige and importance. Their prayer was that I would make a difference in this world by harnessing my intelligence, energy, and my extremely active imagination. Their unconditional love instilled within me a belief that I could attain whatever goals I set for myself. School was easy; I breezed through it. I became a pianist and won every competition I entered. My parents had their idea of my life and I had mine.

Since youth, my desire for total freedom has remained. I want to be free to be me, to live life to the fullest by experiencing all that life has to offer – travel, the ability and opportunity to stand up for my beliefs and to pursue all my wildest dreams. Life was meant to be a joyous, exciting, pleasurable adventure. I wanted to be rich and I had tremendous drive, energy, ambition, and huge dreams. I wanted to get to work and start making my fortune.

I married my high school sweetheart, and set about making my dreams come true. We started a trophy and engraving business and purchased our first home. I got a job at a local bank and had our son Lanny within the first two years of marriage. As the reality of responsibility set in, I abandoned my huge dreams. We were barely making ends meet on one income. I was depressed over our finances.

When our son was six weeks old I was introduced to network marketing. I immediately understood the concepts, and ran with it. In so doing, I rekindled my ability to dream. We then had our second child, our daughter Elise. Our vision was to be millionaires by age 30, and we were well on our way to achieving it. Then, the unthinkable happened. My husband was in a car accident. Ten days later, he died. In an instant, my whole world crumbled. I was a 23-year-old widow with two children. I felt mentally, emotionally, physically, and spiritually abandoned.

My focus was temporarily redefined while I healed. I continued to pursue my banking career and made parenting my primary objective. I was addicted to drugs and alcohol; I was anorexic and bulimic. I never lost focus on my children, but I was in danger until Bert Olson came into my life. He helped me get treatment and find a better way to achieve my dreams. In 5 short years, I was well on my way to recovery and we divorced. Since then, I have had two transitional marriages, one of which allowed me to become the #1 representative in a Network Marketing Company in Canada.

Network marketing can be a powerful tool in the restoration of hope, vision, and dreams in people's lives. It offers equal opportunities for everyone. It does not discriminate in any way; age, gender, level of education, and religion are of no consequence. The desire to rise above mediocrity, and a willingness and ability to learn and teach others the concepts of product ad business are all that is required.

Regardless of what we choose to do in life, we will be faced with many challenges and adversities. Psychology has proven that we will achieve that which we intend, or focus on. The choice is ours. We can focus on the donut or the hole, the cherry or the pit. We can choose to believe in our ability to succeed by focusing on our dreams, goals, and deepest desires, or we can succumb to the challenges by focusing on the setbacks, the naysayers, the uninformed, the lazy, or those who are simply afraid to see you become successful. Network marketing is a legal and ethical form of entrepreneurship that is practiced by moral upstanding citizens throughout the world. If this opportunity appeals to you, grasp it, hold onto the vision, internalize it, and run with it. I am on a mission, a crusade really, to wake people up to their life, their purpose, their potential, and their reason for being. I have the vehicle to facilitate the realization of dreams.

We live on the most amazing continent on the planet, a place where we can virtually be, do, and achieve whatever we desire. This is free enterprise. Yet, the majority of people are trapped and enslaved in a world of scarcity, lack, and limitation. We can choose to be a victim or a victor. Countless times I could have succumbed to the overwhelming circumstances of my life, but I didn't. Today, I realize that every relationship, marriage, situation, and circumstance are cumulatively great blessings. The valleys of my life have proven to be enlightening. I accept full responsibility for all that has occurred, and I am accountable for my destiny. We are each blessed with unique gifts and talents. It is our responsibility as individuals to wisely use these gifts to create the life we desire, inspired by our dreams, in pursuit of our goals and vision. We can live vibrantly in all facets of life: mentally, emotionally, physically, and spiritually. My mission is to teach and lead by example. Whether male or female, we are all equal, powerful, creative individuals, fully capable of achieving whatever we desire.

Everyone's dreams are valid. In a marriage or partnership, on numerous occasions I have witnessed a power and control struggle. One partner may think that they are doing more than the other. Perhaps one thinks that their goals and dreams are more important than those of the other, and then the blame game starts—STOP IT! Take ownership of you; take responsibility for you. Set your life's goals by deciding what you really want. Then, take positive action toward your dreams and goals. What legacy do you want to leave behind? My goal is to be a catalyst for freedom, worldwide equality, and prosperity, and I know that I have the power to reach that goal.

ↄ Betty Anderson

Stop! Look! Listen!

Mary Gale Hinrichsen

My life is great. I am financially secure, I have good health, I am educated, and I have a wonderful family, yet I struggle with depression and anxiety. To overcome depression I stop for a minute, look at my thought life, and listen to that small voice within.

At times I have an article deadline to meet, but because of my depression my efforts seem so fruitless. That makes me think that I have nothing to offer. So I want to give up. But when I take time to stop for a few minutes, look for ways to help others, and listen, that small voice within inspires me to write one more sentence that might encourage or strengthen another. When I help others, it brings me hope as well. Have you ever started a project, a new business, or a hobby? Remember how difficult it was at first? But later, you were inspired to complete that project. Where did that inspiration come from? It likely came when you stopped long enough, looked at what was on your heart, and listened to that small voice.

Stop: Find time to be alone

Look: See what is on your heart

Listen: Hear and follow that inner voice

Once we have those three beautiful basic steps intact, our friendships can thrive, our finances can become secure, and our dreams can be fulfilled. Anything that we want to achieve is possible when we are willing to put forth the effort to stop, look, and listen.

So Stop! Look! Listen! What is that small voice within saying about the future? What dreams and desires are yet to be fulfilled? Stop stressing and start believing that we have been given everything needed to succeed. Start looking for ways to receive by listening and following that small voice within.

ꕥ Mary Gale Hinrichsen

Is Your Highway Clear?

C. John Yeo

There was a highway given to you when you were born, and at that time it was perfect and clear. You see, this highway is the light of life, great white spirit, or God, whatever you believe it to be. The light of life is a highway to the great universal mind, which is all-knowing, always present, omni-intelligent, and all-encompassing, with unconditional love for you.

Do you let that divine love in and allow it to permeate your whole body?

Do you use your highway regularly to help you to find your purpose in this life?

When you have a problem, do you travel along your highway to ask for help?

How do you use your highway? It's yours to use whenever you like and for whatever you like.

This light of life comes from the universal mind to your subconscious mind, and then to your conscious mind, where you can create whatever you want. The more you think about what you want, the more your subconscious mind will work toward your desires.

You see, your subconscious mind never sleeps. It does not reason or know right from wrong. It accepts everything as truth and works on everything from that position. So, if you don't like the way your life is going, you must first change your thinking.

Look at your life like a movie. You have a light source (your light of life), a continuous film (your thoughts and feelings), and a screen (the outward part of your life as seen by others), the way you live. If you do not like the way your life is going, change your film. It's up to you to create the life you want. Visualize what you want and how you want to be. Impressing this on your subconscious mind becomes your new film, and therefore your new life.

This power within grows stronger as you let it work for you. Meditate and listen for the things that can come to you. You will find your life changing toward the life you have created with your inner power.

To start, the best thing you can do is love yourself. Love yourself a little more each day. Look in a mirror, into the pupils of your eyes, and say (with a sincere loving voice), "I love you, I love you, I love you." Do this for 21 days. If you miss one, start the 21 days again until you complete 21 days in a row. I know you will feel happier and more loving. Remember your subconscious mind is the most powerful thing in the world, and the power within loves you unconditionally, always, no matter what you do.

Some of the big obstacles that clutter your highway are fear, jealousy, hate, judgment, negative thinking, self-doubt, and the word, "can't." All of these things block the power from doing its creation with you. Fear freezes you from going forward in your life. I do not mean the uneasy feeling you experience in your stomach just before you perform on stage or sing a solo—that's a good fear and it helps you give a better performance. This is the nameless, faceless fear of your own ability; the fear that cannot stand the light.

Jealousy is self-destroying and a weakness that must be overcome. You do this by first loving yourself until you overflow with love, and then you give that love to others.

Hate does more harm to you than to the person or thing you hate. The person may never know you carry hate for them, so while they are enjoying their life, you have the uneasy or nasty feelings and ill-health that hate causes. It's better to bless them and move on in your own life. If you think you know what the word "bless" means, look it up in the biggest and best dictionary you can find. You may be surprised; I was. Notice how many good things there are in the word "bless."

To prove how powerful your mind is, give yourself a little test:

Be somewhere by yourself and think of someone or something you hate. After thinking about this for 30 to 60 seconds, note how your body feels. Now, relax and think of a pleasant scene, such as a seashore, lake, or mountain. Next, think of someone you love, and after thinking about them for 30 to 60 seconds, note how your body feels. Which feeling do you like? Note that neither of the people or things were in the place you were; it was all a result of your thinking.

Do you spend more time thinking about your failures or your successes? How easy is it for you to think of some failures; name them! Now, think of some successes. Which is the longer list? Golf is a great game for anyone, young or old. Most golfers talk a lot about their good or great shots, but rarely talk about the bad ones. Why not try this in all areas of your life? Practice thinking about the good shots—successes and loving moments in your life. You will feel so much better about yourself if you practice positive thinking throughout your life.

One of the greatest things you can do with your highway is to share it with someone you meet and to whom you are attracted. Make your cake together; a wonderful, rich cake. The ingredients are all the great things that each of you bring into the relationship mixed into a big bowl, the world. You each gradually add flour, which is the love you have for each other. This mixture is blended with milk, the liquid of life. Everything is blended in a gentle and loving way until it is all mixed and ready for baking. All the ingredients and each of the steps yield a beautiful, perfect cake.

When, as a couple, you're ready for true love, you arrive at the moment when you enjoy each other beyond belief. This is the icing on the cake, the lovely pure white royal icing. All the blending and romancing is well worth the time it takes to make your cake, before the icing.

It's difficult to do the icing before you have a cake. Later if children come along, tell them about their highway. Teach them the love of their inner power, and show them how to love themselves and build their own cake. Teach them to ask their power within to help them succeed in all areas of their lives.

Whether you use your inner power for good or bad, is up to you. Whichever you choose, there will be consequences. Therefore, be careful of the thoughts you think and the words you speak.

I hope you keep your highway clear and that you receive all the love, happiness, health, and wealth you desire.

These thoughts are dedicated to my late wife Ollie Yeo, who headed The Alphagenetics Hypnosis Centre of Calgary since 1975. I learned most of these truths over the 12 years, 9 hours, and 20 minutes that we shared together. Thank you for sharing in Ollie's teachings. With light and love, John.

C. John Yeo

The Power to Change

Steven E

Life is always changing. No matter what else may happen, you can count on change. For many, change is quite stressful. One of the most stressful of all changes is finding a new career. Perhaps you've been working just to survive and work has become boring and dull. If you are currently in a job you do not like, take time to work on what you enjoy, and set a timetable for making a change; be patient with yourself. You know there has to be something better out there for you, but what?

I suggest you reach deep into your soul and find that power within; sit quietly and think of what you like to do; things that brighten your day and make you smile; those things you would gladly do not for money, but for pure enjoyment. The answer is simple. The power to change lies within each and every one of us.

Begin finding a path to freedom in your employment. Be sure to have as many options as possible, and develop other income-producing ideas. This will grant you flexibility and self-empowerment. Assess your talents and gifts. Find out what you really enjoy and what you do exceptionally well. Learn what they are and develop your inner gifts.

Once you have an idea of what you would like to do in life, write it down. Each morning, meditate or pray on the things you want. Feel and see what you want, see and feel yourself already having it. I believe you can do and can be whatever you desire in life, if only you believe—and know that you can. You must visualize.

Visualization is something I have written about many times. Because of it, I have manifested more love, joy and material abundance than I could have ever imagined. Let me explain how this works.

We all have experienced a time when we thought of something and, "Bang," there it is. Everything you see was first a thought and then it became the chair that you are sitting on, or a pencil or a table. You must visualize everything before it becomes a physical object. The architect visualizes the house before he picks up a pencil; the poet hears the song before she writes a single word.

Wake up… Live the Life You Love, A Power Within

We all have the power within us to change and make our lives better. Start taking action right now. Be patient. Things always take longer to materialize than we expect. Remember that when changes come about, you have the choice to create fear, or to face the challenge with courage and faith. The only way miracles will enter your life is if you allow them in and believe that they are in your life.

I believe in you and I know that you can have whatever you want in life. Have faith in yourself. Faith is a gift, a gift that is a great power. It is a power in each of us that can literally change our lives.

Steven E

You Can Get There from Here: The Steps to Success in Your Career and Your Life

Barney King

Have you ever watched a baby taking those first few steps? It's a truly remarkable event, and it can teach us a lot about a much larger event: our journey through life.

The baby starts standing in one place, "Here," to be someplace else, "There." The desire to get from Here to There is so compelling that the child is willing to put up with repeated failure and pain. By trying, falling, getting up, and trying again, the baby shows passion, drive, and determination. This process teaches us that nothing is really insurmountable when the objective is compelling enough.

But as an adult, you can't just go from Here to There on desire alone. You have to clearly define where you are and have a compelling picture of where you want to go.

To define *Here*, you have to know yourself. This means describing and fully understanding your core values, talents, personality traits, learning style, and fears.

Your Core Values

What is most important to you? These are the fundamental building blocks of who you are as a person. They can be anything from health, honesty, commitment to service, self-respect, independence, or faith in God. They may relate to the people in your life: your spouse, children, or coworkers. They might relate to activities: work, fitness, service, or school. When you are clear about these values, write them in a notebook. That's the first step.

Next, you must prioritize them—from number one to the end, with no ties. At some point, there will be conflict. Time, money, and resources will be limited, and priorities should be established before the conflict comes up. You must always be certain, in the inevitable trade-off, which values have the higher priorities.

Your Talents

Next, it is important to understand your personal resources. This is also an exercise in finding and acknowledging the truth. Most of the time, your talents are in line with the things you really like to do—things in which you become so involved you that you lose track of time. But you have to be realistic. For example, I like to play basketball, but I'll never be good enough to play in the NBA. I'm over 50 and have a bad back. So it's unwise for me to list "playing basketball" as a talent and then allocate precious time to enhancing my basketball skill.

The first part of the talent search, then, involves looking at what you *do.* Examine your school, life, and work experience to identify those things at which you excel. You might have been pretty good at being a soccer coach. Or, perhaps you enjoy distilling complicated information and communicating it in a way others are able to use.

Next, look at what you *know.* For example, you might know a lot about history, or a specific kind of history, like car racing. You might know different computer languages. Or you might know the regulatory aspects of drug development. It is important to identify all of the areas about which you are knowledgeable.

At the intersection of knowing and doing is usually the key set of potential talents to exploit in your life and career. Align these talents with the list of core values from the exercise above and write them in your notebook.

Your Personality Traits

An area that many of us ignore—because it is just too personal—is an understanding of our personality. Probably the most well-known assessment is the Myers–Briggs test. Various versions of the test can be taken and scored online. The results can help you better understand how you approach things and how you respond to new people and situations.

Your Learning Style

A step beyond understanding your personality is understanding how you learn. Some people learn best by reading and studying charts. Others learn by listening to tapes or instructions. Still others learn by doing things with their hands. Once you have figured out your learning style, you can make sure that you find and process information in that format.

Next, you need to apply the same exercise to those around you. Perhaps reading a thick book with lots of detail is the best way for you to learn. But if, for example, your boss is a bottom-line person and wants quick answers, handing him or her that thick book would be a mistake. You need to provide the information in the format that is best for your boss. Perhaps a single-page summary with lots of bullets and white space would be the right answer.

Your Fears

We are all afraid of something—probably lots of things. The sources of those fears might be small (spiders or bacteria) or big (hurricanes in the Gulf). Sometimes we fear things outside ourselves, such as auto accidents, or thieves and sometimes the fears are within, like fear of changing careers or fear of rejection.

A paralyzing fear for most people is the fear of failure. Others fear success. Marianne Williamson expressed this powerfully: "Our deepest fear is not that we are inadequate. Our deepest fear is that we are powerful beyond measure. It is our light, not our darkness, that most frightens us."

It is important to be honest about your fears and their effect on you. Any change, or attempt at personal growth will be accompanied by fear. When you understand this, you can achieve personal power by controlling your reactions and channeling the fear into choice and action. If you plan to get There from Here, growth, challenge, and fear are inevitable. Since they can't be eliminated, you must trust yourself. Then your decision to act will propel you to where you want to go: to There.

Once you have worked through the self-knowledge process and have a better idea of what *Here* is, it is time to look over the horizon and figure out where you want to be. Remember the baby who was learning to walk? No matter how many falls intervened, the baby was ultimately successful. As you ponder *There*, that's the kind of drive you want to create. Your determination must be based on a vision. Whether the vision is for your personal life or your career, it needs to be so compelling that it draws you forward and pulls you to the future.

As a start, answer some questions:

What is your mission in life?

How do your values, talents, traits and learning style contribute that mission?

Considering the roles you play in life, what do you want to do, have or accomplish?

What do you want to be remembered for?

These are serious questions and require serious consideration. They may call for meditation, brainstorming or praying. These exercises need to be performed separately for both your personal life and your career.

The answers to these questions become your goals. But just identifying them isn't enough. Goals need to be stated in terms that make them SMART: <u>Specific</u>, <u>Measurable</u>, <u>Achievable</u>, <u>Relevant</u> to your career and life, and <u>Time</u>-<u>bound</u>. Your goals take you from Here to There. As with every other step in the process, write these in your notebook.

So far, you have come to know yourself better, identified a vision, and written some goals. Now it is time to do something; to TAKE ACTION.

Start by re-tuning your attitude. Exude self-confidence, a sense of control, and enthusiasm. Engage in positive self-talk, verbalizing audibly or silently the beliefs that will inspire you. Then match your action to the beliefs, thus reinforcing them. That will propel the next action step, and the next, and the next. I can't emphasize enough, though, that without action, all of the positive self-talk in the world won't work.

Take personal responsibility for your actions and their consequences—both successes and failures. If they are *your* actions, they are *your* consequences. You may fear making mistakes. But you have to acknowledge and accept mistakes, even celebrate them. If you aren't making mistakes, you aren't trying hard enough. The key is to learn from your mistakes, to not repeat them, and use them to move to the next level. Rather than being fearful of mistakes, greet them for what they are: opportunities to learn and grow.

The reason you make your goals measurable is so that you can periodically check your progress.

On your journey, you will constantly encounter change. You must embrace change and make it your friend. Let the small steps lead to bigger, more important, more meaningful change.

At the end, getting There from Here is about answering important questions:

Who am I? What do I stand for? What am I good at? What do I want? What keeps me from getting it? How am I going to get it? What actions do I need to perform to get it? What am I going to do today? What am I going to do now?

When you act on those answers, you create your future—using your power within!

Barney King

My Story of Hope: A Life Transformed by God's Love and the Gift of Glyconutrients

Shanda Benson

Darkest before the Dawn

I have experienced three major transformations in my life. My purpose in sharing my story is to inspire those of you who have been through struggles of your own and to offer you hope.

I grew up in New Mexico with my mother. I had two older sisters but they didn't live with us much. I never knew my father. Most of my childhood memories are of being in trouble, of anger, violence, of verbal, physical and sexual abuse. I couldn't do anything right and I hated school; I would have described myself as unwanted, unloved and a stupid failure.

After I completed the ninth grade, we moved to Alaska. Three months into the tenth grade I dropped out of school and ran away from home. I never returned. I continued to make every possible bad choice for a young lady who was trying to numb the pain of the past and looking for love in all the wrong places. Through all of my hurt I became a lying, drug-abusing thief. At the age of 19 I had an abortion, which killed the only child I would ever have. My life was a constant struggle. Every time I started to get things together, I would make another bad choice and everything would fall apart. I had fulfilled my own belief system about myself and my prospects for the future seemed very dim.

A New Hope and a New Beginning

On October 19, 1980, I experienced my first and most important life transformation. I was 20 when I responded to God's love and call on my life. I was "born again" in a moment of faith, but it has taken me 28 years of walking with God to recover from all the damage done living the first 20 years without Him. In all of my struggles to overcome my self-destructive wounds of the past, God has shown Himself to be faithful. I have not already achieved all that He has for me but I hold onto His promise: "He that has begun a good work in me will be faithful to complete it."*

The new year of 1981 was the beginning of my second life transformation. I met Damian and we were married July 18th that same year. We moved to Oregon in 1985 to help start a church. I continued to grow in the Lord but I really struggled emotionally dealing with the grief and baggage of my past. I tried just "putting it all behind me" to become that "New Creation in Christ," but it was not as simple as it sounded. I learned to look good on the outside with all kinds of good works, but inside I still felt empty and unlovable. I called it being "the hollow chocolate bunny."

In 1989, I was diagnosed with fibromyalgia. I had always dealt with health issues, but now the rug had been pulled from under me. Our lives were completely changed! My emotional pain grew dim compared to the chronic physical pain I endured. Some days were worse than others, but they were all bad. We ended up leaving the ministry and all of the dreams and goals we once had. Damian worked, took care of me, cleaned the house, and put up with all of my negativity. Frankly, I wasn't much fun to be around.

Despite all my self-destructive behavior, bad attitude, and failing health, this man continued to show me unconditional love. Through it all, he never complained. He stayed by my side and truly fulfilled his vows, "For better or worse and in sickness and health." By April 1998, depression and hopelessness had overwhelmed me. I truly wanted to die. I was tired of hurting and being sick all the time and I felt like such a burden to my husband. I carried with me a letter that stated, "Do not revive me if I am in an accident; please let me die." I was in desperate need of my third transformation. Once again, God's love and mercy came through just in time. I was introduced to glyconutrients in June 1998 and over the following nine months I regained my health and quality of life.

From Drop-out to Leader

Out of the ashes of pain and suffering a new life was born, along with a purpose and heartfelt mission to help others. Before I got better, my focus was surviving the moment. Now I have big dreams and goals for the future. I had no way of knowing where my path would lead. I didn't know anything about health and nutrition, but I had my own testimony and a passion to help others, and I found a wonderful company with life-changing products.

I attended all the company training sessions and listened to every conference call and audio tape that I could. I learned how nutrients support our body's own ability to heal itself. I went from being someone who was a flunky and a tenth grade drop-out to being someone who not only could learn, but also could teach others. I became a Wellness Consultant. I named by business Daily Manna International because this is my "daily manna" for health and wealth, and I want to share my story with the world. That is how my journey as an entrepreneur, motivational speaker, and author began.

I have learned that my success is more about personal and spiritual growth than about building a business. As I continually apply myself to become the person God wants me to be, He is faithful to lead me and direct my path. Glyconutrients are my daily gift from God. Through them He has restored my soul, health, hope and even my family relationships. It is my heartfelt desire to inspire personal and spiritual growth in others. I teach people about disease prevention and am able to offer hope to those who are already suffering as I was.

The Years that Almost Weren't

The past eight years, which I almost missed, have been amazing. My friend Pam always says, "Don't give up five minutes before your miracle." I almost did, but I found out that God had plans for a future and a hope for me.**

A New Way of Thinking

I have come a long way from the depressed, discouraged, and emotionally disabled person I was back in 1998. I have surrounded myself with leaders and mentors who challenge me to stretch myself in areas I never thought possible. I feed my body with glyconutrients, my spirit with the Word, and my mindset with inspiration. I have invested in my education by attending numerous leadership training events. I have developed a massive library of books and tapes by wonderful speakers and authors. These include Bob Harrison, Brian Klemmer, Robert Kiyosaki, Jim Rohn, Zig Ziglar, John Di Lemme, Jeffery Combs, Paula White, Beth Moore and Dani Johnson. I desire to walk in the ways of the wise and to share that wisdom with those who might be encouraged by my story.

I have changed the negative messages from my past with positive affirmations and goals. I have found my Why, and this is the person I am becoming. I am well known and respected in my business community. I have positively impacted the lives of thousands of people and have been recognized for many levels of achievement. I do whatever it takes to overcome challenges and I empower others to do the same by my example. I have a clear focus and I am a leader. I live with enthusiasm and passion, and I inspire others to do the same. I enjoy traveling the country as a guest speaker and author, sharing my Story of Hope and teaching about Wellness and Glyconutrients. I know that I am making a difference by sharing all the gifts that have been shared with me. I am very thankful and want to give God all the Glory, now I do my best to live my life on Purpose with Purpose!

* Being confident of this, that he who began a good work in you will carry it on to completion until the day of Christ Jesus. (Philippians 1:6)

** "For I know the plans I have for you," declares the LORD, "plans to prosper you and not to harm you, plans to give you hope and a future. (Jeremiah 29:11)

Shanda Benson

A Song in My Heart

Shelli Frances

At the tender age of three I knew there was something magical about singing, and by the reaction of all who observed, there was a magic about how *I* sang. I looked for every opportunity to sing – family gatherings, grammar school glee clubs, church, and high school choirs. I auditioned for solo parts and participated in a beauty pageant with a talent competition when I was 17 (which I quite unexpectedly won). At age 20, I began singing at churches and spiritual music festivals. By 21, I was the lead singer in a local top 40 band. I knew I had found my true calling and continued singing in various bands. I had arrived; It was just the beginning. Or was it?

I'm sure I wasn't the only 21-year-old who had heard a well-intentioned parent or family member say, "It's time to grow up and put childhood dreams away," or "Get a real job, something stable with benefits." My mom, Fran, said: "Take a good typing course or get a job with the telephone company." Looking back at that time in my life, I have to laugh.

Well, in keeping with family tradition, I soon found myself no longer singing for my dinner, but married and a new mother. I kept telling myself, "I'm being more responsible." What I was really doing was allowing everyone else's voice to rise above my own inner guidance. It left me feeling torn, confused, and unhappy. As a result, I suffered deep depression.

By the time my daughter Kati was five, her father and I had divorced. I *tried* holding "regular" jobs but found that my depression was getting the better of me. I started doing day jobs to pay the bills, and singing at night just to make the day jobs tolerable. I guess you could say my music was my "Soul Pay." The exhaustion was overwhelming at times, but I couldn't bring myself to let go of the music. Somehow, I always found a way to do both. Everyone thought I was crazy and sometimes, so did I. But each time I stood up to sing, I knew everything was right with my world. I felt every tone, every vibration – it was as necessary to me as breathing.

Years later I gave birth to my second daughter, Cameryn, on my own. Well, I wasn't really on my own, her big sister Kati tag teamed

with me every inch of the way. My band and the regular gang at the local country music club, where we had been playing for years, "had my back" when I had to stop working three weeks before delivery. In fact, the night I gave birth to Cameryn, a guitar player's wife called the hospital hourly to broadcast reports to the crew and audience. They were with me emotionally every second of my labor. The next day the lead guitar player came to see me at the hospital. With a big grin on his face and a tear in his eye, he presented me with a dream fund that had been collected in a cowboy hat from everyone at the club. This was my ticket out of central California and they knew it. It was as though they knew my special bright light was rapidly fading and it was then or never.

In January 1996, I packed a U-Haul and my girls and drove to southern California with our dream fund. Kati was twelve and Cameryn was one-year-old. I started from scratch. We lived in a one-bedroom apartment in a terrible neighborhood. Within a week I landed a job with a "house band" at a local nightclub, three nights a week. Kati would watch Cami while I worked at night, and I would be with her during the day. Soon I got job offers from other bands and within a year, I was making a living (although a modest one) just doing music. I continued to seek my "big break," and several times thought I had it. However, I had another reality to face. I knew that I wasn't 25 anymore and because of that, it would be harder to make anything happen. I finally decided that I wasn't going to let that hold me back.

I figured out a way to get to Nashville to record a CD of original songs. There was **one song** on that CD that I really loved and felt connected with. I have since offered regularly to perform this song for charitable events in support of battered women's shelters, teen mental health, and suicide prevention, among other causes. As I continued to market the demo, I met a great producer in Los Angeles who instantly "got it." He offered me a recording contract with his independent label. Four days before we were set to sign a multi-million-dollar deal the devastating events of 9/11 occurred. Everything stopped. Frozen funding forced the record label to go under. Locally, corporate events were canceled because no one wanted to get on an

airplane to come to San Diego! My local performance calendar completely cleared out.

At that point, I took a HUGE step back! I went inside myself and took a deep breath! What was all of this *really* about? I reexamined my life, my intentions, my purpose in the world, and my priorities—everything! It took almost 4 years to get my life back on track. As the saying goes, "Until we are ready to learn the lesson, it keeps repeating itself."

What I have come to know for sure in this journey called "life" is that it brings both blessings and challenges. I also believe that the true miracles of our life often come through our greatest trials. Six years ago, I recorded *I Will Shelter You* in Nashville with the intention of launching my singing career. What I've now come to realize so many years later is that this song was quietly waiting in the wings of my life to be utilized, not just for entertainment, but as a path to comfort others, honor the human spirit, and provide help for those less fortunate. This song was never intended to be about me.

I originally recorded the song from the emotional space of a single mother sheltering her young daughters from the hurricanes of life, to let them know that I'd always be there for them, no matter what. From there, the song has now taken on a life of its own. *I Will Shelter You* is now an international fundraiser, from which, the majority of the proceeds go to disaster relief, on the heels of what we all witnessed in 2005.

I Will Shelter You sings of the hurricanes of life and the compassion and love within each of us to shelter one another during difficult times. With the help of everyone who hears this story and joins in to help, we can change lives beyond what we could ever imagine. Yes, I am a singer with a dream; it's just not the one I started with when I was a girl of three. When is comes down to it, what we give away is what is most important.

Shelli Frances

The Day After Christmas—A Different Gathering

Linda R. Uihlein

As an active volunteer Emergency Medical Technician (EMT) in my community, I have witnessed some powerful life lessons. One of these lessons took place on December 26th as I was sitting comfortably at home with the wood stove warming my chilly old cabin. I was hoping for a quiet day with no more emergency calls from our community at Christmas time. How selfish can I be?

The pager toned and I was intently listening for the address and the type of emergency—cardiac arrest, CPR in progress, about a mile away from my cabin. This house was about 30 minutes away from the hospital. I had a sinking feeling—the day after Christmas and a serious call.

Still, there was always the hope that this patient would be revived and go on to live a productive life. Perhaps in their excitement the family was mistaken and he had just fainted. I shifted into my spiritual and emotional rescue mode. I use this mindset to stay in control during calls. Every Rescuer has his or her own way of dealing with the emotional toll rescue work entails. Both career and volunteer rescuers enjoy their work but we have to create our own ways to deal with the stress and pain. If not, we can suffer burnout and want to leave rescue work.

As I drove to the house I was rehearsing the sequence of the scene size-up and patient assessment. I needed to review on my way to the rescue because as soon as I arrived I would be in "automatic." This is the best way I know of working in an environment where I have to rely on my training, experience, and intuition.

When I arrived on the scene, well ahead of the other Rescuers, I noticed several family members crowding around a young man lying on the living room floor in front of the Christmas tree. A family member was performing cardiopulmonary resuscitation, CPR. I knew we would have to work together for at least 10 minutes before more advanced care arrived. When I do CPR I seem to be in a world all by myself, yet conscious of the world around me in a surreal way. I did the chest compressions as the family member did the artificial breathing; as I was counting the compressions, I would

cue for the breaths to be given. CPR is a team effort and we worked well together.

While concentrating on my rhythm, I still had time to reflect on the room and its occupants. Even though I was busy with a life-saving procedure I had to stay aware of my surroundings. We were truly on our own without advanced professional help for the short time it took the fire company and rescue squad to arrive. Family members talking near us were imprinting Tony's name on my subconscious as they were quietly discussing the situation.

I looked across Tony and noticed the unopened gifts still under the Christmas tree, waiting for the recipient to arrive. I will never forget the gifts and the questions that flooded my mind (Who were these for? Is the person in the room? Will the person forever remember the medical event instead of Christmas and its meaning for the rest of his life?). It is interesting what goes through your mind when you are in a highly stressful situation.

Soon other family members and friends began to arrive at the house and to crowd into the room. I was fairly new to the community but soon became aware of my name being passed among those present. I was baffled about how they knew my name, since I did not recognize anyone. I was hoping the fire company would arrive soon. I knew Tony's best chance of survival lay in the Advanced Life Support that was on its way to this rural area.

During this time I overheard stories about how Tony was loved and respected by family and friends. I also heard stories about Tony's kindness being shared throughout the room as we did CPR. What a true blessing he must have been to everyone who shared his Life. This was the first time I was privy to such an interaction with a family while performing CPR. This made the plight of Tony even more personal.

The other EMT's started to arrive and they began more Advanced Life Support on Tony. We all worked as a coordinated team. The seconds seemed like minutes and the minutes seemed like hours until Tony was placed in the ambulance. December 26th would hold a certain sadness for all in the room instead of happiness and peacefulness the day after a holiday brings.

Only later, as I was leaving, did I recognize my neighbor, Mary. She came over and thanked me for trying to help her brother. Other family members, still in disbelief, thanked the Rescuers for coming to help. I will never forget this call. I will never forget the family in their grief thanking those who tried to help their family member. This brings out the real meaning of thankfulness and how precious life is. It was not long before I thought about the general well-being of my family a thousand miles away. How lucky I was!

I feel both humbled and honored to be a part of a volunteer fire company helping our neighbors when they call for help. Everyone has a unique gift he can share with others. That sharing has the power to save and to change lives. I hope I can continue to help others for many more years. The experiences impact every aspect of my Life.

Some calls will always be remembered.

Editor's note:

The names have been changed in this true story.

Linda R. Uihlein

The Environment for Results

Dewitt Shotts

"Far better is it to dare mighty things, to win glorious triumphs, even though checkered by failure, than to take rank with those poor spirits who neither enjoy much nor suffer much, because they live in the gray twilight that knows not victory nor defeat."

— Theodore Roosevelt.

Results occur when someone takes responsibility and makes them happen. Outstanding results occur when, instead of listening to others or to that negative voice in our minds, we focus on the results desired. The results person asks himself, "What is needed right here, right now?"

Ideas are easy; it's acting on them that is the problem. It's the difference between actions and stories. Henry David Thoreau once wrote, "If you have built castles in the air, your work need not be lost; that is where they should be. Now put the foundations under them."

Self-concern is the killer of results. Eleanor Roosevelt said, "You must do the thing you think you cannot do." We get too caught up in the details of how, where and when to create results instead of focusing on the result. Self-concern has stopped more progress than any other human failure.

Roosevelt also said, "the future belongs to those who believe in the beauty of their dreams." Everyone is creative and the failure to act because you are afraid of how it will appear to others has killed more dreams than any other thing in life. As Emerson said, "Whatever you do, you need courage. Whatever course you decide upon, there is always someone to tell you you are wrong. There are always difficulties arising, which tempt you to believe that your critics are right. To map out a course of action and follow it to the end, requires some of the same courage which a soldier needs."

You must be devoted to the result and go after it. That devotion, and the courage that must accompany it, is the power within each of us.

Dewitt Shotts

PUSH a Little or a Lot

Kathleen Hudson

PUSH: Pray Until Something Happens. I rely on my spirit a lot. It's that little piece of me that sets my course each day, moment by moment I talk to God. Prayer is my strength, the underlying current in my passion. The relationship that comes with this simple form of conversation is so special that it is difficult to describe. I pray until I feel spiritually full and freed from worry, doubt, and aggravation. Prayer allows me to be loved unconditionally. It took some time to realize just how important this simple form of communication is in my life.

In 1994 I was a victim of the down-sizing of a local bank. I had been an employee there for 26 years. I had worked there through my child-bearing years. My house payment, credit cards, and children's savings accounts were tied to that bank. I had medical conditions that were stress-related, due to my job. I could not believe my employers could so easily toss me aside. My father had worked 45 years at the same job before he retired. I grew up in the 1950's and remember hearing the advice, "Go to school, get a good job, and keep it." Loyalty to my job and longevity in the workplace were my ideals. I could not understand being treated in such a way.

I had to stir my inner power in a hurry. I was floundering on what to do next. How would I pay the bills? What would I do with my time? In the first month, I had my house clean by 10:00 a.m. I hated soap operas and was bored by noon. The most difficult part of this time in my life was not having structure in my day. If I napped, I could not sleep at night. I overate to soothe the frustration and boredom. I longed for summer vacation, so I could spend time with my terrific kids.

I finally decided to go back to school at 45. I knew at that age it would be a difficult task. I decided to go into the field of insurance and investments. The state insurance exam was fairly easy for me. However, learning about securities was a sincere brain challenge and I did not like it. Also, the idea of selling to make a living made me nervous and I wasn't sure that I could be successful. I began to pray for something to take the place of this newfound madness. I yearned

to do something creative. I was suffocating in securities laws and regulations. I wasn't even allowed to send out a card during the holidays without getting an approval. This was not my style.

I wanted to be free so I decided to start my own business. After all, I would not fire myself! I'd be safe again. Sometimes when we pray, answers come in the most unusual way. As I started out, I felt that I was being directed every step of the way and my confidence began to grow. I was running a business and actually doing it successfully. Since then, I have started several businesses and each one provided a new learning experience and income opportunity. I made my fair share of mistakes, but I also made progress with each one.

There is a saying, "Iron sharpens iron." I didn't understand that at first, but I do now. I have co-partnered my business with another "difference–maker." We have combined our skills and talents to make a difference in our world, helping others secure affordable and safe housing. I'd like to say I am able to help others, and I can use my creativity to do it. The power within me spills out in what I do. I create possibilities for people who feel hopeless. I have come up with a compelling sales pitch that engages others to jump on my bandwagon and help. I have discovered that as you help people fulfill their dreams, blessings flow out to you in the process.

Today I am the executive director of the Homes4Heroes.org Business Alliance. We help those who serve our public by getting them discounts on service fees and retail items. We provide free gifts to those of them who qualify and who are new homeowners here in Arizona. These are people who serve our communities on a daily basis, risking their lives defending us against fires and lawlessness. We also serve educators, clergy, and government workers. These are wonderful people who take lower paying jobs because they want to make our communities better. Our communities work because they do; they are dedicated servants.

I understand the commitment of those public servants. Those principles were instilled in me as a child. I have prayed, waited, and thanked God for all the little wins in my life. I understand that I can be involved in prayers being answered for others. To me, this is using the power within to come full circle, flowing to touch all areas of life.

I love what I do now. Today I could write a thank you letter to the "powers that be" at the bank for letting me go. Since the downsize, the bank has changed names three times. With the many mergers; it's unclear to whom I should send it. I didn't understand for a number of years why things happened as they did. Now I know that my struggles and successes over the past 10 years put me on the path of awakening and tuning in to the power within for answers and acceptance. It's all good now.

ꕥ Kathleen Hudson

Embrace Silence

Dr. Wayne Dyer

You live in a noisy world, constantly bombarded with loud music, sirens, construction equipment, jet airplanes, rumbling trucks, leaf blowers, lawn mowers, and tree cutters. These manmade, unnatural sounds invade your sense and keep silence at bay.

In fact, you've been raised in a culture that not only eschews silence, but is terrified of it. The car radio must always be on, and any pause in conversation is a moment of embarrassment that most people quickly fill with chatter. For many, being alone in silence is pure torture.

The famous scientist Blaise Pascal observed, "All man's miseries derive from not being able to sit quietly in a room alone."

The Value of Silence

With Practice, you can become aware that there's a momentary silence in the space between your thoughts. In this silent space, you'll find the peace that you crave in your daily life. You'll never know that peace if you have no spaces between your thoughts.

The average person is said to have 60,000 separate thoughts every day. With so many thoughts, there are almost no gaps. If you could reduce that number by half, you would open up an entire world of possibilities for yourself. For it is when you merge in the silence and become one with it that you reconnect to your source and know the peacefulness that some call God. "Be still and know that I am God," says it so beautifully in Psalms of the Old Testament. The key words are "still" and "know."

"Still" actually means silence. Mother Theresa described silence and its relationship to God by saying, "God is the friend of Silence. See how nature – trees, grass – grows in silence; see the stars, the moon and the sun – how they move in silence. We need silence to be able to touch souls." This includes your soul!

It's really the space between the notes that makes the music you enjoy so much. Without the spaces, all you would have is one continuous noisy note. Everything that's created comes out of silence. Your thoughts emerge from the nothingness of silence. Your words come out of this void. Your very essence emerged from emptiness.

Those who will supersede us are waiting in the vast void. All creativity requires some stillness. Your sense of inner peace depends on spending some of your life energy in silence to recharge your batteries, remove tension and anxiety, thus reacquainting you with the joy of knowing God and feeling closer to all of humanity. Silence reduces fatigue and allows you to experience your own creative juices.

The second word in the Old Testament observation, "know," refers to making your personal and conscious contact with God. To know God is to banish doubt and become independent of others' definitions and descriptions of God. Instead, you have your own personal knowing. And, as Melville reminded us so poignantly, "God's one and only voice is silence."

Dr. Wayne Dyer

Awaken to the Dream

Stacey Rousseau

Isn't life about enjoyment? I often see vivid examples of life just passing by, being wasted, of people who are struggling and spending most of their time merely surviving. Living in a cycle—running to and from obligations—seems to be the norm. What has happened to "stopping to smell the roses," or enjoying the small things? Isn't it true that life can become so complicated so quickly, especially in an ever-evolving world! Some people have plenty of money and some have plenty of time; rarely does anyone have both. Is there a way to get the enjoyment out of life that we really should? Can we actually dictate our own lives and have the lives we've always dreamed of?

Sometimes it is easier to dismiss a goal or dream instead of putting forth the effort to pursue it. On the other hand, perhaps you've tried a venture or business that you thought was going to change it all, but it just didn't turnout. Well, a past failure is no reason to stop pursuing what is rightfully ours—the life and lifestyle we want for ourselves and our loved ones. We can all have the freedom to spend valuable time with our children, to share our time with our spouse, to pursue hobbies we've always put off, and even to be asset rich with no time obligations on Monday morning!

Allow me to ask you a few quick questions. What exactly would you do with your day if you had no financial burdens and life was at your feet? You would probably choose something other than going to work. Do you feel as though you are living each day to the fullest? Are you receiving and experiencing all life has to offer? Why did you buy this book?

A few short years ago, I was in a similar place. I was spinning my wheels in corporate America, trying to figure out how the dots would connect. I worried about how I could maintain my lifestyle, add children to the equation, and be able to stay at home with them. It just wasn't happening! Out of pure chance I took advantage of a luncheon to learn about a business option. I have no idea what made me ask to tag along with my coworker, but it turned out to be the most important decision I have ever made!

The more I learned about that business, the more excited I got. I just couldn't think of a reason not to do it! I decided to make a commitment to changing my future, mainly because, quite honestly, there weren't many other options! I had gone back to college to finish my Associates Degree, and decided to pursue a Bachelor's Degree. I figured it was the only thing that could get me something different than what I had. My corporate job had some nice perks, such as railroad retirement, profit sharing, and health care, but I knew the stress and hours that came with it were more than I could handle for the next 35 years! Not only that, but each and every day the corporate structure of business is changing and becoming less and less secure. Let's face it: job security is a thing of the past.

Most things in life are actually quite easy. The difficulty lies in making the decision to execute them. It can be a scary thing to step out of the norm and to abandon security and comfort. But consider never changing, not growing, staying stagnant. To me, that is not the path of life. The "path of least resistance" brings little fruit. Go for it! Live it up and live up to your potential! I decided that this would be my vehicle to help me achieve all that I had dreamed for myself; all of the things that I had lying deep inside me waiting to get out! I had always felt that there were things inside of me, great things, which I couldn't quite identify. They were big things to pursue and achieve but I never could quite determine what they were or how to pull them out. It was as though I was born with a mission and it was my duty to find it and fulfill it. Nothing I had pursued gave me the feeling that I was on track until I put myself in this business.

This business vehicle has led me down many roads, all of which have given me gifts. The most important of these is growth. I have expanded as a person. I have become more open and knowledgeable, more personable and likeable, and more logical and rational. I am a better parent and partner; I have been given abilities that have changed my life forever. I have much more control of what happens in my life; I know what my future will bring. You see, we are the masters of our lives. We determine our circumstances and we get exactly what we ask for. So it is in our best interests to condition ourselves for growth, for prosperity and freedom. It is about reaching inside and finding your best. You must have a plan; a way to get what you are seeking. You can feel the fulfillment!

This is exactly what I have focused on and I am moving forward to build an international, award-winning champion team. It will be a group of people who are focused and determined to make a change and a difference. They are willing to step out and be above average and to have the courage to break out of the rut. I have focused on creating a step-by-step system for my teammates to follow to build their businesses to their desired level. I am ever grateful to my personal business coach, who opened my eyes to life and I am now dedicated to assisting my team to achieve their peak potentials.

You too can make a change and a major difference in your life. Reaching deep inside yourself, finding that power within, will allow you to put aside your fears, think outside the box and become the master of your life, and with that, enjoying the incredible fulfillment that is long overdue.

ꟷ Stacey Rousseau

Everyday Is Saturday

Sam Crowley

"Is tomorrow Saturday, daddy?" asked my 4-year-old daughter Madeline. "No," I replied, "Why do you keep asking me every night if tomorrow is Saturday?" "Because that's the only day we have fun together," she replied.

I knew exactly what she meant. I was 36-years-old and had spent the past 15 years working my way up the corporate ladder, the last 5 in a management capacity. Monday through Friday I would leave before Madeline woke up and would arrive home sometime around the dinner hour, just in time to kiss her goodnight. Sundays would consist of going to church, and then sitting around the house with a knot in my stomach waiting for Monday morning to arrive. I thought I was doing what I was called to do—be a provider for my family. I was certain that Madeline wouldn't notice me being gone most of the week anyway. My wife, Angela, could raise her until she was 7 or so, then I would have made it to the mountain top of my profession and be able to spend time with my children. I was positive Madeline loved her daddy and talked about me all the time when I was gone. I was convinced that my business success had also transferred to the home.

I remember traveling on business one week in 2004 and calling home to check in. I asked Angela whether Madeline missed me and was asking where daddy was. Angela's reply shook me up. She said, "It's really no different when you travel; either way you're never home Monday through Friday."

It dawned on me that I had missed Madeline's first four years and was about to do the same with our second daughter Laura, who was two months old. I was addicted to my work, spending all my time and energy leading a sales force, chasing quotas year after year for people who could not have cared less about me and my family. Many people in my position would've sucked it up, never entertaining the thought of leaving a six-figure executive level job. Many would've said, "Only 8 more years till I retire," or, "It's a good paying job, and they did give me a 2% raise last year." But I knew I was different.

I had grown up the youngest of eight children in Bradford, Pennsylvania, a small city with a population of 10,000. My father left home before my first birthday, leaving my mother to raise eight kids on her menial nurse's salary. I remember how I thought that food stamps were the only way one could purchase food at the grocery store, because that was the only way my mom would buy groceries.

I had a debilitating stuttering problem until I was 14 years old. I used to call my friends and hang up the phone when they answered because I couldn't ask a simple question like, "Is Mike there?" I would hide under my desk at school, hoping the teacher wouldn't call on me to answer a question. Now you can't shut me up. I have a story to tell and I am on a mission to help anyone who prefers freedom over security. I realize that life is not a dress rehearsal, you get only one shot. I have given up the gossip, greed, and egotism of corporate life for the comfort and joy of my family. My focus has shifted from being a C-E-O to being a D-A-D.

I'm reminded of the story of a bear in a zoo in New York. The bear was not adapting well to the zoo and would never leave his 12-by 12-foot cage. He had been prodded and poked with sticks by unkind patrons. The New York Zoo found a home for the bear in Germany. Its new home had acres and acres of space over which he could roam. But when the bear was let out of his cage he simply paced 12 feet forward and 12 feet back, as though he were still confined to his cage. That was me. I was in my own mental prison, never thinking I could do more than exchange hours for dollars. I would give everything I had to the company that signed my paycheck and leave nothing for my family when I got home each evening.

Then it hit me—I could do anything I wanted! I could enjoy the life God intended for me to have if I just stepped out in faith. The first thing I did was start a Christian home-based business with the hopes of making money and spending time with my family. The business has exploded and I haven't missed one dinner with my wife and kids since leaving corporate America. Prior to leaving my job, my daughters wouldn't even leave the couch to kiss me good-bye when I left the house. Now I can't go to the grocery store without hugs and kisses that last for ten minutes. I almost sacrificed a lifetime of that love for corporate politics.

Many of my friends and co-workers used to say, "Wow, Sam, you really know how to motivate and inspire people. You should be a public speaker. You should write a book." Well, guess what—I now share my story with many organizations in the Cincinnati area and envision traveling all over the country speaking to people who are like I used to be. Those people are working at a j-o-b (**J**ourney **O**f the **B**roke), getting paid what the position is worth, not what they're worth.

So here I am. The stuttering kid from Bradford, Pennsylvania, turned motivational speaker and coauthor: The executive who had a job most Ivy League graduates would love to have; the sales manager who went on quota-buster trips and stayed at the nicest hotels. Most importantly, I'm the father and husband who figured out before it was too late that every day could be Saturday.

ꟸ Sam Crowley

Are you a Drummer or a Dreamer

Jasmine Sampson

There are some beliefs that I hold passionately. They are not "head" knowledge, but heart knowledge. They infuse and shape every aspect of my life. One such belief is that each of us is a unique and precious gift to this world. We come into this life with a dream or dreams that are uniquely ours. We come with a purpose, with something that only we can give to the world, and a particular set of interests and talents that equip us to fulfill that purpose. The tragedy is most people live in a way that leaves no time to discover those gifts, fulfill that purpose, and live that dream.

I once attended a jazz concert. I was sitting next to a man of about 50 who was entranced by the drummer. Throughout the drum solo he was tapping along and shifting in his seat, totally alive. During the break I asked him if he was a drummer. All of the life that had been vibrating out of him a moment before suddenly disappeared. He collapsed back in his seat and said, "Oh, I'd like to be, but no, I'm too old." This man oozed rhythm. It was clearly a gift and a passion. When he was drumming, even in his imagination, he was alive. I would be willing to bet that when he was 8 years old, he wanted to be a drummer. Maybe he was lucky and made it to 14 before he gave up on that idea because he had to "be real" and earn a living. He had buried his gift, and so he had buried his life. Too many people live life like that drummer.

We live in a world where we think it is normal to spend our most productive years working 40 to 60-hour weeks, and being too tired and too busy to spend any quality time with our families—let alone develop any real interests or passions. We've come to believe that dreams are unrealistic, and that being adult means being a slave to a job. What sort of craziness are we accepting as normal? The mindless consumption and universal dissatisfaction that I see around me is a result of people who are divorced from their souls, from their dreams, and from their purposes. The world needs more drummers, and it needs more dreamers.

I remember my father as a gentle, wryly humorous man. He was a self-effacing presence in the background of my life. On more than one occasion my mother told me how, several years before I was born, she had persuaded him to leave the family business and to seek something more suited to his natural talents. When he broached the subject with my grandfather, he was told that to do so would mean that, should anything happen to him, my mother and brothers would not be provided for. Although my mother was willing to take the risk, my father was not. He continued in the family firm but was often ill. He died some 10 years younger than his relatives. At his death I had an image of him as a piece of watered silk that had remained crumpled and dirty at the back of a dark cupboard. Because he had spent his entire working life in employment that did not express his natural gifts, his beautiful and subtle "coloring" had never been seen. There was something he had to give to this world that had never been given. That story and those memories contribute now to the passionate desire I have to empower people to live from their giftedness.

All my life I have wanted to make a radical difference in the world. When I was a little girl I dreamed of being rich and living in a beautiful home with beautiful gardens. Poor people, ragged and sick, would come and be made well in my home, and when they left I would give them bags of money to take with them. They would arrive miserable, sick, and poor and leave happy, well, and rich. It was a powerful dream and, many nights I took it with me to sleep. It is a dream that I am living today.

As an adult I recognize that it is not only the financially poor who are in need. As I look at the world around me, I see that there are four key areas of poverty or lack in this Western culture: lack of Meaning, lack of Finances, lack of Time, and lack of Health. I believe all four are necessary for abundant life.

I believe that this world is dying because so many people are living too fast and working too hard to discover their purpose on earth. I believe that assisting people to reconnect with their spiritual purpose and to fulfill it is my particular gift. My personal goal is to empower 100,000 people worldwide, with Time and Financial

Freedom. I want to assist them in identifying and developing their gifts and living the dream that is in them. I want to help them fulfill their unique purpose in life. I know that when people live with a sense of purpose they live with excitement, passion, and enthusiasm. If enough people do that, the world will be changed.

Our gifts may be obscured but they are never dead. There is in each of us a Divine Spark that is always seeking to express itself. I believe that there is a Divine Dream of Justice and Equity, Freedom, and Peace that is struggling to be born on this wonderful, beautiful, pain-wracked planet. I believe that an essential and unique aspect of that Dream is held within every human heart. I believe that the possibility of living that Dream—of giving our unique gift to the creation of a transformed world—is within our grasp if we will only take courage and time to look.

I believe that finding and fulfilling our purpose is not optional, it is essential if our planet is to survive. Only knowing and living our Purpose will satisfy the hunger of our spirits, which expresses itself now in unsustainable consumerism. Only peace in our hearts will create peace in our world. Our world needs more drummers and more dreamers. Our world needs you and your Dream.

∽ Jasmine Sampson

Catch the Ball!

Gregory Scott Reid

One of the key ingredients for success can be summed up with one simple word—Focus! On what? That's easy—one thing at a time. You see, in this fast-paced, "multitask" society we live in, it seems we are judged by how many different things we can do all at one time; yet in reality, we can do only one thing well at any given time.

Imagine being on your computer playing music, checking emails, and working on a Word document, Excel worksheet, and PowerPoint presentation, while looking up stuff on the Internet. Your system might move pretty slowly. Right? Guess what? The same applies to us. We can do things faster and better, if we focus on only one thing at a time.

To illustrate this point even more, I want to share the following example with you.

It's fourth down, 12 seconds remain on the clock, and your team is down by three points. You are the wide receiver in the biggest football game of your life, and you are called upon to win the game for the sold-out crowd. You line up to begin the final play. The ball is snapped and you run down field.

As the ball is heaved in your direction, you feel the anticipation of the event which is about to unfold. You envision it all in your mind, step-by-step, move-by-move. You know exactly what is going to happen.

You catch the ball, tucking it in close with the outside arm to keep from fumbling. You are going to twist left and then right, throwing the defenders off guard. As more people run your way, you see yourself spinning to the side and dodge one close call after another, while jumping over the opponents like they are nothing more than simple obstacles.

As you soar into the end zone, the gun explodes, ending the game. Your team is victorious. They rush the field and hoist you upon their shoulders. The crowd goes wild, chanting your name in unison.

Later that night, you will be the talk of the town. Everyone wants to have a moment of your time to tell you, "Great job!" They want

to shake your hand or pat you on the back. This is your time to shine! All the years of training and hard work have finally paid off. All eyes are on you. You are the man of the hour.

Then Bam!

Your mind brings you back to the moment. You were lost in your imagination. You lost focus and redirected your thoughts and energy. As the pass arrives you juggle it like a hot potato, letting it slip through your hands.

The crowd goes silent in disbelief.

The only thing you hear is a voice inside repeating one of the coach's basic lessons, "Before you can do anything else, you first need to catch the ball. Until you do that, everything else is pointless."

Now, let me ask you—are you catching the ball? How many things are you juggling in your life?

Learn to focus on one thing, master it well, and then move on to another. *Focus* may be the missing ingredient in your recipe for success. Focus is the power within.

Gregory Scott Reid

The Millionaire Woman Tells the Truth about Life Success

Beverley Johnston

Live and love when you have the option; when it stares you in the face; when you see and feel it in your heart. It is in these moments that life has meaning.

Why do I do what I do? I do things because I know I can. It comes from a trust that going through the process creates the essence of my existence. Each of us has a gift to offer, every day. Each gesture we give today will somehow, and in some way make a difference in someone's life. Sometimes it is a universal gift given to whom we may not know. When the time is right, someone will wake up and capture the gift to enhance a life. They, in turn, will pass that gift on to other people.

I feel a huge responsibility to partake fully in my life. When an opportunity arises, I have been known to say, "I will find a way!" A saying I read years ago has always stayed with me: "Awareness is the freedom to choose."

I remember as a child staring at the snow-covered mountains far in the distance and hearing stories of skiing. That world was not available to me, but my desire to one day experience it stayed with me. I traveled to Europe when I was 24 years old and worked in a ski village. The magical world of the snowy mountains in winter finally availed itself to me and I learned how to ski. My desire to ski freely like the wind down the mountain intensified. Returning to Canada, I decided to become a great skier. At that time a friend had signed up to stay in a ski cabin at Whistler, but had to give her place up in the group. I said, "I will pay you for your spot and take it." That event changed my belief in possibilities. I persevered with tenacity, commitment and passion. At every chance, I drove the two hours to the mountains and skied. I took lessons. I skied with the group, skied with new skiing friends and skied alone. Each day I improved just a fraction more in my technique and performance. I skied whenever and wherever the group went and I skied as hard as I could and

as long as I could. They offered me technique tips like, “face down the mountain;” “follow the rhythm of the land.” They critiqued my equipment; “your poles are too long,” “change your wax today,” “face the fear, but value your life.”

There were falls and aches in muscles that I never knew existed. There were days that my feet were so cold I wasn't sure I would make it safely to the bottom of the ski run. There were days of glorious sunshine, flying like the wind down a slope with friends who were doing and feeling exactly what I was. There were days that I spent most of my time falling into the soft white powder. Once I realized what I was doing wrong, I would have the most exhilarating float down the mountain side, being one with the rhythm of the powder and the slope. It took me three years. I still remember standing on the top of Whistler Mountain, and feeling totally exhilarated and yelling as loud as I could, “I did it, I am a great woman skier!” That next run had such a feeling of joy and freedom to me that I always cherished that memory and it gives me strength when the daily living events of my life are a challenge.

I grew up as an overweight child. In physical education classes in high school this created a problem. In my mid-twenties, I decided to shed my extra pounds and start running. I hired a health consultant and a running coach. I persevered, walking, running; gasping for air and then running as if the breath was a part of my forward movement and the legs were light and in rhythm. It took three months. I lost 25 pounds and felt the joy and freedom of running for the first time in my life. This also began my path to living a life of healthy food choices and a lifelong interest in healthy living. When I run, I love the feel of the wind across my face, blowing through my hair. It is a wonderful sense of freedom.

Next, I set some running goals and trained for a 10k run. I remember it as if it was yesterday. It was my first of many 10k races over several years. I met terrific people and shared wonderful experiences. I reset my goals and ran several half marathons.

One spring day, while on vacation at Whistler Mountain, my world was plunged into chaos yet again. All it took was one wrong turn on a steep slope. I had two surgeries and three pins in my leg

and endured a long recovery time. The deformity was frightening. I was determined that I would run and ski again. It took one year to be able to run again and it took two winters before I could once again ski. My passion for sports and my love of the outdoors allowed me to regain the same confidence I had prior to the accident.

Several years later, I challenged myself to stretch my realm of possibilities to run a full 26-mile marathon race. I figured out my possible time to complete the race, wrote it down and placed it on the dashboard of my car for one year. It took practice, time and perseverance. I continued, because my heart was totally committed to run that race and finish within the time I had set. I ran because I knew that I could. In 1991, at the age of 42 years, I crossed the finish line in Portland, Oregon with a smile you could not miss. My finishing time was within four seconds of the time that I had stuck on my dashboard a year before. The mind can create powerful things if we allow it to. I have completed eight marathons and five one-half marathons since then.

In the late nineties, I decided to stretch my boundaries. I entered the world of triathlons. Running was my best sport of the three (swimming, biking and running). I invested in coaching. I trained and practiced continually on all three sports. I completed several small course triathlons over the next year and a half.

I was inspired by friends who had just completed a race called The Ironman Triathlon in Penticton. I quit my long-time job at a children's hospital and I had the time to train for the huge race. An Ironman race consists of a 2.4 mile swim, a 112 mile bike ride and a 26.2 mile marathon to be completed in 17 hours. I was committed to the race and signed up along with some friends. We hired coaches for all three sports and joined a triathlon club where there were several people doing the same race that we were training for. I trained constantly for a year, stretching my time and my distances in each sport until I was prepared to go the distance required.

Race day came. I had one of my best swims ever that day. Biking was my challenge of the three sports and I was extremely happy about my amazing results. I set out on the run knowing this was my passion and my best sport. At mile 3.5, pain set in my lower back. It never went away and increased in severity no matter what I did.

Ice, rest, walk or sit—nothing helped. I pushed through the pain to stretch myself to go the distance and to complete my dream of running under the coloured glass chandelier at the finish line.

As I learned later, I passed out at mile 21. I woke up six days later in an Intensive Care Unit. My twin sister, who had been my support crew in the race, was told I had very little chance of surviving. She was told to call my family. She refused to let me go. She kept repeating, "You are healthy, you can do this, you are not ready to die." To this day they call me the "Miracle Woman" when I go to Penticton to visit and volunteer in the medical tent as part of the team at the yearly Ironman events. According to medicine, I should not have lived through that night.

I was trained well, I had prepared my mind well, and I had taken care of my body nutritionally for years and particularly the last 2 years before the race. Everyone wanted to know what went wrong. Medically, it was "hyponatremia" and some related complications. The question to me was, "What went right?" I know that my body was fine tuned right down to the cellular level. I have always known in my heart that I would live to be a wise older lady and be blessed to share this wisdom to empower others.

I knew from somewhere deep inside, that I was too young to die. I was not ready to go and I had to live no matter what the medical staff was saying. Thanks to all of my friends and family, I won the race of my life that day. Three weeks later, unable to breathe very well or walk very far, my dad, twin sister and I walked across that finish line under the chandelier and we cheered, laughed and cried with joy. My question to you is, "What fine tuning are you doing in your life to survive the unexpected?"

My stories let people know how I have lived my life. My intent is that they may empower you to consider that strength inside of you. Use it to create a meaningful life for yourself and for the people whose paths you cross each day.

ᔓ Beverley Johnston

From Despair to Victory: How I Reinvented Myself

Bruce M. King

In early April 2002, I was days away from my fiftieth birthday and found myself out of a job and seemingly out of viable career options. In the seven years since I had left a twenty-year Army career, three salary jobs hadn't worked out and I had failed three times at starting new businesses. I was humiliated and frustrated, and I knew I was failing my family as a provider. Our lifestyle had expanded with the previous jobs, and we were financially over our heads. We were growing deeper in debt each day and were heading for financial disaster. I was asking myself tough questions. Should we sell our house and move to a much smaller one? Should I just get whatever job I could? My wife had been amazingly patient with my career adventures, but was now pleading with me to establish myself in something.

I looked around at what jobs might be available for a guy my age, but in my mind, nothing seemed to work for me. I knew I had a lot to give, but I wondered if I could ever again find an employer who would recognize my potential, give me a chance, and reward me adequately for my contribution. Every day I prayed that I could find something that I could do that was meaningful and profitable. One day I got a call from someone named David, a mortgage broker, who wanted to talk to me about a position as a loan officer. The bad news was that the position was based solely on commissions and my own marketing. I had tried and failed three times previously as a salesman, so this wasn't a thrilling interview. I knew that being a loan officer had to be very complicated, and I knew nothing about mortgages. I also discovered that getting paid would take weeks, maybe months. Loans didn't usually close for weeks or months. Just the same, the idea of being a loan officer was intriguing, so I took the job on a part-time basis. Meanwhile I worked part time in another sales job, hoping that between the two positions I could survive.

The first few days of this career reinvention was an emotional time.

Each day I prayed for wisdom to learn the business and courage to go out and make myself known to potential clients. As I looked at all the forms, the loan program guidelines, the regulations, the rate

sheets, and all the complicated procedures, I realized that becoming a first-class loan officer wouldn't be an overnight event. I compensated for my inexperience in the industry in two ways. First, my energy level was higher than that of anyone else in the office. I worked evenings and weekends and I spoke about mortgages to everybody I knew. Second, I decided that I would stick to my values and treat my clients as I would want to be treated. I would listen and make recommendations based on the client's best interest, not on my income needs. I vowed that I would not recommend unnecessary loans.

Things slowly began to happen for me. When I stumbled at my first attempts to get loans, I picked myself up and tried again. As I started prospecting for mortgage leads, I found that the people skills I had acquired throughout my life really made a difference. People wanted a mortgage professional they could relate to; someone who empathized with them and didn't put pressure on them. I found that many of my competitors were overly concerned about making large commissions and not too concerned about returning phone calls or telling their clients the whole story. I found that as a loan officer I had the power to bless people's lives, to help them purchase homes, to ease financial hardships, and to improve lifestyles. I really enjoyed helping people purchase their first home.

After about six months, I realized that with a full-time commitment to the mortgage business I could make a breakthrough, so I quit my other position. I felt inside that this was "it," the chance to be myself and be a winner. Although I was green in the business and had so very much to learn about loan programs, mortgage terminology, and customer service, my ability to develop customers and get referrals grew. I began to build a real excitement for the future and an enthusiasm to help as many people as I could. Within weeks, my income began to grow faster than I had even hoped. Excitement swelled inside my heart, as I knew I had discovered a vocation that resonated with me. I can't describe the warm feeling of satisfaction I felt, knowing that I had finally found my groove.

During my second year in the mortgage business I began to realize that I had reached the limit of what I could do by myself as a loan officer to grow my business. I also knew that there was a higher level of service I wanted to provide and I wanted to help more people. I needed to further reinvent myself. I needed to discover how to hire the right kind of people to work with me to increase my business and yet maintain the qualities that made me distinctive as a loan officer. I needed an assistant that could help handle the volume of phone calls and administrative responsibilities. I needed people to meet with clients and help meet their needs. Such changes, I found, are not easy. Finding the right people, training them, and leading them, as part of a well-coordinated team was a huge challenge. After several failed attempts to find a suitable assistant, I ran across a fine young man named A.J. He and I resonated well as a team and our business together exploded. Before long, we needed to hire more assistants. A few months later, I invited Kathleen to join the team. Kathleen is a networking phenomenon, a tireless worker, and a loyal business partner. She came on board and super-sized everything we were doing. As the team increased in members, we felt the growing pains, but eventually learned to operate as one.

All this has added up to more success and satisfaction than I had dreamed of. All of this was the result of an unexpected opportunity and the application of my inner power. That power is my unique God-given gifts and talents, along with the skills gleaned from a half a century of life experience. I want to prosper even more so I can have opportunities to give back to the world. I know I will need to further reinvent myself, for change is an eternal state. Now, I know that I can rise to the occasion.

ᘓ Bruce M. King

Favourable Winds of Change—the Opportunity of a Lifetime

Simon Harris

In 1991 I was a builder. The work was interesting because many of the projects were on older, listed properties, and at that time the market was buoyant. However, the long-term prospects were likely to be poor, as the work relied on continuing physical stamina and a continuing buoyant market. I was looking for something. At some point, I fully intended to become self-employed. What kind of self-employment was somewhat vague, but I had a dream; embryonic, directionless, but nevertheless a dream.

During that year my parents were in New Delhi, India, where my father was in his last job before retirement. I had the opportunity to do a six-month solo overland trip through 21 countries to India, where I visited my parents. It was truly a life-changing experience.

In the process, I had the privilege to be the first British tourist in Iran since the revolution. I nearly got shot in Pakistan and came down with dysentery in Peshawar, where I was looked after by American Ophthalmologist Herb Freeson, who had established the Noor Eye Hospitals in Kabul, Afghanistan. I then worked for Mother Teresa in her Home for the Destitute and Dying in Calcutta. Finally, I came home from Nepal with Paratyphoid fever, bad guts, a new dream, and plenty of time during my recovery to take stock in my future.

During that time my dream was growing, becoming enriched, and focussed. I deliberated for five more years and then in 1996 finally plucked up the courage to embark on a course to retrain in the field of medical support. I took a biomedical science degree, but also had ophthalmic dispensing as a vocational safety net. The field of optics really interested me so I went on to get a second degree to become an optometrist, which is what I still do.

The university experience showed me that it is possible to pursue a dream and succeed. I had not had the opportunity to get a degree at the "proper time." I know now that the proper time is whenever you do it—when it's right for you, when the door is opened for you.

I love being an optometrist. I enjoy working with people instead of machines, and I enjoy knowing that I am making a difference, daily. But the story does not end there. The educational experience had stretched my horizons. I was dreaming of greater things, bigger achievements, and higher goals. I was introduced to network marketing by Christian friends in summer 2005. I immediately realised the potential to gain financial independence. It meant me being my own boss and I could do it on a part-time basis. I was buying into a business with a system.

The products I initially chose to become involved with were ethical and health-promoting. I use them still, although I have recently moved to another company. With my new company I believe I can impact the lives of many, many more people. At the time of this writing, this company is the sixth fastest growing small business in the United States. This business will provide me with a residual income and, therefore, the freedom to pursue higher goals, such as supporting or establishing community projects or overseas schools, orphanages, hospitals, or eye units. I can do whatever my imagination and passion might produce.

The most important thing about my new business is that it has challenged my "poverty principle." Many people just want enough to "get by." I believe this comes from the belief that we don't want to work ourselves into the ground in a humdrum job. Many people are employed in fairly boring jobs and they're satisfied with a decent day's work and getting by. But with the predicted increase in the number of people drawing pensions (the first of the retiring baby-boomers), many will really be struggling. It is possible that, for some, old age will not be a happy time. Many will struggle just to live and will be unable to pursue any dreams. I do not want that.

As a Christian I feel compelled to make a difference in the lives of others. I want to have the freedom to do that. I will continue to serve my local community and beyond in the field of optometry, but with my extra income I can do much, much more. What my network marketing experience really has given me is the ability to

vocalise and reinforce my WHY. This is of paramount importance for those who want to succeed. My WHY is my defining purpose in life—why am I here, what am I going to achieve, what my dream is. It has allowed me to see into my future and visualize myself as being successful. I am establishing various dreams with increasing confidence. As I live in the hope of this WHY and reinforce it habitually on a daily basis, I find my life changing. I am banishing negativity, embracing hope, and looking to a higher attainment. I am leaving the old viewpoint behind like a worn out garment that does not fit anymore. My circle of friends is slowly shifting to include those who also dream of great things, bigger achievements, higher goals. It's amazing that these people just seem to pop out of the woodwork as my enthusiasm increases. This WHY is a key factor in success because it gives a focus. It is a focus that will change and expand as my dreams are realized—a sort of "WHY in flux." So, you see, the WHY itself develops as we grow; it is a dynamic that is constantly shifting upward.

By actively pushing away as many negative influences from my life as I honorably can, I feel I have cast off from a shore to which I have been tethered far too long. This is an awesome freedom and it unfolds almost daily. I'm moving upward and inward. As C.S. Lewis said, "If you're not aiming for the bullseye, then in truth you won't be too disappointed if you miss the board altogether." For many people this is the stark and tragic reality of life.

I have a dream. In my heart I have already fulfilled it and I am actively living it. I heartily encourage you to do the same. If you want a copy of my WHY as it stands at the moment, then, by all means, call me. Think big; think "impossible;" think impossibly big. Embrace it with your soul, write it down, vocalize it as you see it in your mind's eye, and speak it back into your life daily. Be amazed at the transformation, and most importantly, pass the secret on.

Simon Harris

Building Wealth For The Masses

Debbie Allen and Patricia Drain

Over the past 30 years, Debbie Allen and Patricia Drain have built more than 17 highly successful companies, selling many of them for significant profits. They did this by using their expertise as business owners, speakers and authors to share any and all information they personally learned about growing their own companies. They believe that they allow small business owners, speakers and entrepreneurs, to move on the fast track to success by sharing what they learned the hard way.

For seven years they dabbled in the event business, occasionally conducting small seminars and retreats together. Then, one day, after Debbie returned from a real estate boot camp in Florida, she called Patricia and told her that "this was it!" They needed to think bigger and turn their event into a boot camp. Patricia was intrigued, but not sold on the idea until she attended another boot camp on Internet marketing.

They both knew that this would be the perfect venue to share what they had learned over their many years as successful entrepreneurs. To make a real impact in people's lives, they understood that they needed to surround themselves with the nation's best-of-the best wealth-building experts for days on end. As they interviewed dozens of possible speakers, they began realizing that the information they would be sharing had the potential to be life changing for everyone involved.

Today, they have developed a wealth-building atmosphere like no other. They both owe their success to taking quick action with fearless goals, developing powerful business alliances, and having an unstoppable entrepreneurial spirit.

Together they created and co-founded Maximizing Success, Inc. Their first wealth-building boot camp was held in Scottsdale, AZ in January 2005. They hoped to have about 100 attendees at their first event. Little did they know that 500 people from Canada, Europe, Australia and Japan would attend. That's when they knew that they where onto something bigger and greater than they had originally imagined.

As the weekend of their first event unfolded, they celebrated their success. The success of putting on such an event was nothing in comparison to the raving testimonials that hundreds of the attendees were sharing during the three days.

Some of the comments included:

"This event is unbelievable! My life will never be the same again."

"Thank you for allowing me to give myself permission to make a lot of money."

"This is the most powerful information in one weekend I have ever received in my entire life!"

The result of their first boot camp was so inspiring they decided to incorporate the business and start filling their calendar with future life changing events. Together Patricia and Debbie have created an environment that would put anyone who attended on the fast track to success and wealth.

These three-day long, morning-to-evening educational events give so much information that it is like attending a wealth-building university in one weekend. Universities and community colleges don't teach people what they can learn at these events. Maximizing Success wealth-building boot camps teach wealth building as an art form by masters and gurus who "walk the talk."

Patricia and Debbie are lifelong learners. To stay cutting-edge with their expertise, they attend many events each year to learn from other experts as well. A few months after their first big event, they decided to attend a smaller one in Las Vegas on how to conduct seminars and special events. What they learned most from attending was that the world is full of people who want to steal your dreams.

After paying a large amount of money to attend, they got on the plane, checked into a hotel, took a cab to the event and sat there like sponges waiting to learn. The two quickly picked up on the presenter's negative vibes. He was not being supportive of their dreams of continuing to develop more wealth-building boot camps. Instead, he was actually trying to steal their dream away from them.

After just a few hours of his destructive attitude, they walked out. They promptly demanded a full refund, something neither of them had ever done before. They promised one another that as soon as

they got their refund money, they would both buy something that would remind them to avoid any future dream stealers.

Debbie bought a small, but perfect diamond that would remind her to never allow anyone to take the sparkle out of her dreams. Patricia purchased a set of Bose noise-reduction headphones to remind her to silence any dream stealer who was not supportive, tried to intimidate or offer the wrong negative information.

Beware: Dream Stealers Are Everywhere. Avoid Them and Go For Your Dream!

Patricia and Debbie continue to go for their dreams, and thoroughly enjoy their new business baby: developing wealth-building events. They continue to surround themselves with inspirational, educational speakers, and experts that are making a positive impact on the lives of people all over the world.

These are two powerful, gutsy women to watch! Together they have an amazing synergy that allows them to develop cutting-edge wealth-building knowledge for the masses.

Have faith in your dreams and you will always have the power to achieve.

ꕥ Debbie Allen and Patricia Drain

Intersection with Destiny... Turning Derailment into Destiny

Teri Werner

I am amazed at the similarities life offers—or rather those we offer life. The dilemmas we face and the principles of empowerment which propel each of us to a place demanding that we face our destiny strike a similar pose and proposition to all of us. The terrain of the path or perplexity that has come into our lives is different for each of us. However, the path providing principles that empower us to forge through our personal traumas and trials remains the same.

In times of trauma, it is natural to think that your "derailment" or dilemma is unlike the experience of others. In truth, we are not as different as we may think. I have experienced the reality of turning derailment into destiny, as you can by embracing your own path through your trials to your destiny. You will find the essence of excellence as you implement time-tested spiritual principles. Eventually, you will find and trust in the truth that has proven itself in thousands of ways and millions of days. There is grace for the place you face.

You may make sarcastic comments about it, hoping that someday your heart will recall it as something to laugh at. Deep within your spirit, you weep. You try to call it by another name, a name acceptable and recognizable. Nonetheless, the truth echoes through the coarseness of it all. It was a train wreck. Who knew that something so traumatizing would bring you to this place, a place that will change the natural course of what you knew to be your life. This is your time and your destiny.

Although your story of perplexity and pain differs, the path to your destiny is the same. The principles that propel all to empowerment and purpose are of paramount importance. This is your focus.

I had experienced dramatic success early in my professional life. However, I came to a place of derailment and desolation through the deception of another. I will not delve into the details, other than to say that I was desperate for a change.

This absolute desperation for change caused me to search for an inner strength. I desperately prayed to God, reaching out with all I had within me. "I know that my only hope is in You, that You have a destiny for me of passion, purpose, and prosperity. I know that You are the creator and author of my life, so you must know the beginning and the end. I will listen and lean on your words to me and follow your path, and do as you lead me. I will not avenge myself. You are my protection and my prosperity comes from your principles, not my own. If your principles work, they will work for me now, or nothing will."

I was known to be a very strong and accomplished woman, yet I felt depleted of my personal strength. I was unaware that I had given my strength to others through my lack of forgiveness. I needed some answers. I knew I needed more. I had to do my part as I felt led to do, and I was willing to do whatever it took.

I soon realized that forgiveness would become a requirement. In prayer, from an incredible place within my spirit, I realized that I had to forgive those who had betrayed me. It was the most difficult thing I have ever done. *Forgiveness costs the forgiver, and is free to the one forgiven*. No matter the cost, it freed me to move forward in faith, fervor, and favor.

Forgiveness produces Faith in God and yourself as well as fervor in moving forward to your destiny, benefiting from God's Favor.

With each day I had chosen pain over power, dilemma over destiny. Those who deceived me were still in control of my life. I had given them the right to control my life, by withholding forgiveness.

In forgiving, I knew I deserved a culture of excellence and I had the power within, through the power of God, to create that in my life. I actively and aggressively exercised forgiveness to those around me. It was not easy. However, I prayed about forgiving, speaking it out, praying it out loud, and writing it down. If I felt it was beyond my power to do at that time, I would ask God for guidance and His help in forgiving. I would then speak a statement of forgiveness over that person out loud. The more pain I felt during this process, the more times I would repeat it out loud.

Knowing that feelings follow actions, I spoke statements of forgiveness whether I believed them or not, felt them or not; I did not go by my feelings, but by the fact that forgiveness was the only way I could move forward in my life. Then, one day, I noticed that I truly had forgiven them. I knew this was so as I felt no pain at all when I thought of them, or when someone mentioned their name to me. I could recall that it had been painful, but I no longer felt the actual pain of the situation.

Unforgiveness produces fermentation of your past, fear of future, and forceful approaches to the relationships and realities of your life. This force causes you to repel the best from you and works against your frantic attempts to achieve positive change in your life.

I did not forgive the others for their good, because their lives were not impacted by my forgiveness. I forgave them for me.

The favor introduced into my life by the power of forgiveness, that God given power within us all, has opened doors for excellence in business and personal relationships. As I speak on spiritual principles in life and destiny-driven business, I am blessed with favor and amazing good fortune. I am blessed on many levels, from international speaking and leadership opportunities to working with and representing high-profile persons. I experience empowerment and promise while being propelled to my passion, purpose, and prosperity.

I am reminded daily of the seeds of forgiveness which have yielded an incredible harvest and the empowerment and peace to move forward.

The same path of spiritual principles and process is available to you. These principles work, no matter the age or stage of your life. Your path is a process. Trust the process. Many choose isolation and procrastinate on forgiveness. In their desire to wait for a more perfect time to forgive, they create paralysis. This creates an excuse to cling to the past, a place of comfort. Choose progress over paralysis.

The rate of progress at which you reach your purpose and prosperity is directly proportional to your pursuit of spiritual principles. There is a plan to prepare you for your destiny with every delay, distraction, and detour. You are at the intersection of your past and your pursuit of spiritual principles, as you desperately reach out to your destiny!

You have the seed of excellence within you. It is vital that you reach deep inside yourself and use that power within, the power, the inner spirit, the force that allows you to forgive, allowing you to turn your derailment into destiny.

ଓଃ Teri Werner

Flip the Switch: Three Easy Steps to Turning on Joy and Freedom

Ardice Farrow

Let's talk about what happens when you flip a switch?

Imagine walking into a dark room. You are carefully feeling your way, unsure and apprehensive that you might run into a piece of furniture. You can barely get around the room, let alone do anything fun or interesting. It's all about survival.

Now, you turn on the light switch.

Wow! You can see. You can move around with ease, find objects, turn on the computer or get a book from the book shelf. All sorts of things that were not possible in the dark.

Your experience is now one of power rather than survival. The room is no longer a threatening dark hole. Now, you can play and create. Your experience of life is altered and expanded.

When you flip the switch, you open up the currents of power into your personal world. Somewhere there is a rushing river and a big dam with generators, churning out power that is just waiting to be used by you. Now you have access to that power.

How does this apply to you personal life?

Most of us want a great life. We all want a life full of our own unique and powerful light. But, for the most part, we stumble through life, hoping that our bright light will come very soon in the near future.

We say things like, "Someday when all of my hard work pays off," "When I get it together," "When I get my ducks in a row..."

We live in the shadows, trying to recover from the suffering of our past, hoping for some idyllic future that will never come. Most of us wait until old age, tragedy or the threat of death wakes us up.

Don't wait for old age, tragedy or near death – you can *Flip the Switch* now. You can go from anxiety and obligation to unbridled, "blow you hair back" joy and freedom, right now.

When you discover the simple act of *Flipping the Switch*, your life, your business, your relationships, and your sense of self becomes transformed.

I am living proof.

For decades I worked to improve myself. I studied, I stood on my head, I meditated, I went back to school, changed husbands, changed jobs, changed my hair color, my wardrobe and the car I drove.

No matter what I did, or how hard I tried, the results were the same. My experience of life was slightly expanded and improved, but I still did not feel good enough. A low level of anxiety and discontent continued to permeate my life. The "shout it from the mountain tops," "can't stop smiling" joy, freedom and confidence that I longed for eluded me.

I possessed a friendly and upbeat personality, so no one had any idea of the monsters that chewed at my soul.

And at one point I gave up all I knew—or thought I knew—and followed my intuition. I began to practice three simple steps and soon found myself standing in the midst of my life with my hand on the switch.

With a simple *Flip of the Switch,* I could turn any situation from dark and gloomy to light and joyful.

It's that easy. At any moment I can choose to *Flip the Switch,* no matter what the situation, or how seemingly negative the actions around me. I can *Flip It* in an instant.

After decades of some success, my financial situation had imploded and was a complete disaster. I was hiding in shame as my small fortune turned into a pile of mounting debts. But, when I *Flipped the Switch* - my so called financial ruin suddenly became a great playground for new opportunities.

I *Flipped the Switch* on my business relationships and gave up blaming, finding fault and resenting my colleagues.

I *Flipped the Switch* on my personal and family relationships which had always been a convenient place to lay the blame for my lack of success. When I *Flipped the Switch,* I could love and appreciate each of them for what they had taught me.

Everywhere I went in my life, I began to try out my new power to *Flip the Switch* and it always worked without fail.

I began to share *Flipping the Switch* with others, and witnessed how the most difficult and chronic situations would alter and transform.

And now I share the three simple steps with you.

After you practice them individually, they come together in one fabulous moment, propelling you forward into a world beyond your imagination.

Step One - Awareness

Hello, hello – anyone home? Wake up!

For most of our lives we are asleep at the wheel and then we wonder why life is running out of control.

Each of us, over time, has created a set of beliefs and a story about the limits and fears of our life. Our every moment becomes a reflection of these fear-based beliefs and the limiting inner dialogue that runs ceaselessly in our heads. We have been lulled to sleep, hypnotized and left powerless by the drone of our inner dialogue. We are so identified with this fear-based conversation and story that we cannot even separate ourselves from these beliefs.

So the first step to *Flipping the Switch* is to begin to listen to our personal dialogue; to listen to what I call the Inner Committee. These inner voices judge everything and everyone in our lives, criticizing our every move, filling us with doubt, resentment and endless excuses and justifications.

When you begin to listen, you will start to distinguish the various voices of your Inner Committee. It will shock you. You will feel like your head is full of a thousand chattering voices all competing to control you, all with something negative or limiting to say.

If you doubt this for a moment, begin to listen to yourself the moment you wake up. What are the first thoughts in your head?

"Today, I have so much to do – I will never get it done. I hate Tuesdays."

"If only I had stayed up late and worked longer. I am so lazy."

"There is not enough time to get the kids ready for school. We will be late as usual."

Some of us have voices of love and power and at times they can be heard over the din of negativity and fear – but for the most part we are held captive by the conversations of doubt and limitation.

So begin by listening – simply listen.

Step Two - Acceptance

Perfectly imperfect exactly as you are.

Acceptance – is the real trick. As soon as we discover all the twisted conversations that dominate our existence, most of us want to judge ourselves. We are full of regret for lost years, guilt, shame, blame or any other version of that oh-so-nasty habit of judgment.

But acceptance is the key. To have the power of *Flipping the Switch* and choosing a life of joy we must abandon judgment.

Judgment, no matter how cleverly or logically disguised, is an act of fear. You cannot live in fear and love at the same time. You must be completely immersed in love and self acceptance.

Judging will sneak up on you. Comparisons will lead to opinions and soon you will be up to your neck in judgment again. It's like quicksand: One false step and it will suck you down and drain the vitality and joy right out of you.

Imagine that we are swans who were raised by ducks. We have suppressed our beauty, strength and our power to soar. We settled for waddling around, quacking and getting all our ducks in a row. There is nothing good or bad about being a duck. There is nothing better about being a swan. It is simply a different quality of life.

When the proverbial ugly duckling discovered it was a swan, it did not have to go to school and get a degree in Swandom or work to be worthy to be a swan. It merely claimed the truth of who it was and was let loose.

So there it is. Once you are aware of the limiting inner conversation, there is nothing to change, fix or improve – just something to accept.

Step Three - Accountability

Hey, you! Yes, you! Now is the moment to Flip the Switch

When you are standing inside of step one and two, you are in position to *Flip the Switch.*

The struggle and effort, the obligation and suffering are gone. There is simply the opportunity to choose what you want—*Flipping the Switch.*

The power of being human is the power to choose, but we have chosen unconsciously for most of our lives. We have created our lives as a reaction to fear rather than a deliberate creation of love.

But it's so easy; with Steps One and Two you have freed yourself to choose consciously.

Choose what you want; choose what lights you up; what puts a smile on your face. With practice, *Flipping the Switch* will become automatic. It will become your second nature.

A grand and wonderful life is not something that will suddenly occur someday. A wonderful life is built day by day, moment by moment in your act of choosing.

Take on the practice of *Flipping the Switch* as an experiment and you will soon discover that all your drama and trauma, your suffering and waiting have disappeared and your life is more glorious, more delightful and more fulfilling than you could have ever imagined.

Simply remember, that in any and all circumstances, at any moment you can "*Just Flip It.*"

Ardice Farrow

Waking Up to Connecting Purpose with Lifestyle

Erofili Stavroulakis

I changed careers in the year 2000 and went from the hospitality and tourism industry, to applied psychology. I began volunteering in many different organizations. I learned a lot and gained valuable experience in my new career, but I was still unsatisfied. I began the further study of the mind–body connection and became interested in Bowen Therapy. As I became aware of my energy, my personality began to change. I began to open up and share with clients more. I was enjoying what I was doing, but I was frustrated with the instability of my income. I realized that I wouldn't be able to support myself and my family, and my future was not secure.

I needed to be around the best—the best minds and the best developments. Sure enough, the universe provided an opening. Within days, I received an e-mail from an internationally recognized entrepreneur, Rod Moore. He introduced himself and his business to me, swinging open the golden gates of the best opportunities. I was totally amazed and overwhelmed to receive this connection. This began my living of almost two months in shifted consciousness of the unknown realms of the world I had asked for. With total and complete amazement of my attempts to absorb and understand what I had opened myself to, I felt blessed and stayed with the process. A link from Rod's website took me into another world. The website link was to "Audio Motivation," operated by Josh Hinds and Andy O'Brien. This introduced me to international movers and shakers with phenomenal prosperity and success. On this website, I came across links to two well-recognized individuals. I had seen those links on Rod's website. Initially, I resisted visiting one of the links for over a week. I don't know why I resisted, but it doesn't matter now. That website has proven to be the missing link in my life—my "Why."

When I felt the time was right, and I was ready, I revisited Rod's website. I clicked onto the link, and that click changed my life forever. My life moved dramatically to another level. Although I felt completely alone in my ignorance of what highly successful business entrepreneurs were doing, and what was available in the world beyond my realm of understanding, I welcomed the new changes.

The link I was avoiding was my switch; it was about my "WHY" and who better than the legendary John Di Lemme, to share this message. Initially, I was interested in how John had overcome stuttering and the motivation behind this driving force. I began listening to the weekly live telecalls of the Motivational Club and ordered a free CD he offered. However, not fully understanding what he was talking about when he said "MLM" (Multi-level Marketing), I was curiously determined to find out more. As my initial interest of John's life story kept me interested in his major adversity, John also spoke about moving forward, living your heart's dreams and overcoming fear. In order to do this you needed to step out and talk to people about a phenomenal business, with the potential to earn a six or seven figure income. This is how poverty conscious I was, because I had no idea what six or seven figures amounted to. I had to actually write out numbers to see the figures on paper. I couldn't believe what he was going on about and how this was possible.

At last, I understood that it was a business he was talking about, but what type of business? The CD contained information that really shook my head. It further convinced me that this was a clear sign for me to stay in touch with his teachings. I listened over and over in the car and never tired of it because it was all new to me. Perhaps I would hear something I had missed before. Convinced and ready to hear more about this "WHY" concept, and connect to this MLM idea, I ordered the *Find Your WHY* CD and then it all happened. I sat in my office and listened. Suddenly, the life changing heart wrenching words, the conviction, the examples, the stories, the certainty, got me right in the heart – deep in the heart, pulling and tugging and aching. I was at a loss for words and in total awe. Tears began boiling up and I began to cry uncontrollably. In total amazement – I nearly fell off my seat. I couldn't sit anymore. I began pacing around and around in the office, still listening. My heart was aching so much that I couldn't believe what was going on and what I was hearing. I thought I was dreaming, the experience was surreal – entirely incredible. This went way over my teachings in applied psychology; this information was so powerful and so raw.

I wrote to John telling him what I had experienced and thanked him for his message. John replied and encouraged me to continue learning and listening to my heart. Listening to my heart's desires and my dreams allowed me to really wake up and begin living my life. I now look forward to living with a future vision. My "WHY" has now positioned me to move toward what I want for myself in life, as well as what I want for my community and the less fortunate.

I'm now getting started and warming up to my new life ahead. To further support my success, I am learning from the world's leading authorities in the industry including Prosperity Teacher, Randy Gage. I am now in the process of building a million dollar board of director's team in order to build a million dollar business and beyond, for myself and for those who are also on the team.

I have truly woken up to the power within. I am on track to living the life I love, connecting my purpose with lifestyle!

Erofili Stavroulakis

Become a Diva and Add Fun to Your Life

Queen Diva Robbie Motter

Have you spent your life working all the time never taking time to have fun? That is how I lived my life for years and years, until one day I was almost killed by a drunk driver. I gripped the steering wheel as I saw a car heading straight for my driver's door. The first thing that came to mind was, "I can't die now; I have not had time for fun." Then a miracle occurred: Instead of hitting my driver's door, the car hit my back bumper, tearing it off and spinning my car around five times. I was terrified, but I was alive.

That day changed my life. I started giving myself permission to add fun to my busy schedule. Yes, I still have a marketing and public relations firm; I still serve clients in government, speak at seminars across the country, am a Business and Life Coach, co-host a television cable show in Long Beach, and serve as a Regional Coordinator for the National Association for Female Executives. Yes, you might say, I still work a lot. But most important, I now have added fun to my life. I accomplished this enjoyable task in a most unusual way.

On February 3, 2005, two California associates, Fannie Green of Perris, and Gisella Thomas from Murrieta and I had the great idea to start the DIVA Registry. Within just a short time, close to 100 dynamic women had registered to become DIVA's. Many of these women were shy, but in no time at all they were attending events wearing their Diva pins, boas and crowns. At each event you could see these shy ladies become more sure of themselves as they would reach out to others. They gained new confidence. As people started coming up to them, asking them about their DIVA pins, crowns and boas, a comfortable and open dialog began. They started building relationships and shared with each other about who they were, what their business was, and how they could help each other.

In March 2005, several of us took Jet Blue out of Long Beach, California to New York. We wore our crowns, boas, and pins, and by the time we arrived in New York, everyone on the plane wanted to have their photo taken with the DIVA'S. That night, The NAFE affiliate network in Brooklyn had a gathering and we all went. We

met a gentleman who was the publisher of the largest on-line New York business magazine. He really liked us and was impressed by the fun we were having. He invited us to attend the governor's St. Patrick's Day Party at the Waldorf Astoria. We accepted. He took us to our table and told us to just sit there looking stunning. He said he was bringing some important people over to meet us. He did just that. We met many important people, and even had our photos taken with many of them. An editor of the largest magazine in Ireland took our photo, and later published it in his magazine.

Women who have become DIVA's have said that it is like magic. They have added fun to their lives, becoming more daring and outgoing. The DIVA pins help them start conversations with strangers. They feel great about themselves and have so much fun wearing their boas and crowns to business events.

The DIVA's do not have organized meetings. When the three founders learn about fun events, they send an e-mail to all the DIVA's saying, "We will be at this event, if you can be there, show up and wear your pin, crown, and/or boa." We go to business events, plays, boat cruises, etc. We have even attended the Oscar and Emmy award ceremonies.

When men started seeing how much fun the DIVA's were having, they started asking how they could join. The DIVA founders put their heads together and came up with a new group called The Top Hatters. The byline read, "If you are a courageous man that wants to deal with outrageous women, become a Top Hatter." Thus, the Top Hatters were born.

Our DIVA's are from many different professions, some are business owners and entrepreneurs. We represent a wide range of ages and many ethnic groups. We all have one thing in common—to add fun into our already busy lives. Each DIVA who joins is allowed to pick her own DIVA name. Many of them already know their DIVA names. Each member gets one unique name and no duplicates are allowed. New members receive a plush bear with a boa, a glitzy DIVA pin, and a certificate with their DIVA name. They also get their photo and a link on the DIVA website.

Here are some fun DIVA tips I've learned:

You can create magic and fun anywhere you go, the key is to SHOW UP.

Carry crayons in your briefcase.

Read funny books and watch funny TV shows and movies.

Share funny stories with your friends and other DIVA's.

Hang out with fun people.

Be daring and do things just for the fun of it.

All you potential Diva's and Top Hatters, come join us! You will be surprised at the new doors that will open for you and the many new friends you will meet. Girls and guys just want to have fun! Truly, you will "Wake Up and Live The Life You Love."

Robbie Motter

Crossing into the Unknown— A Journey of Adventure

Audessa Siccardi

Finally the long-awaited letter had arrived. My heart was filled with excitement, yet common sense warned me that something was terribly wrong. I tore open the sealed envelope. My eyes scanned the black letters, searching for the good news that had kept me waiting in Amarillo, Texas, for three years.

I read it so quickly that my brain could barely register the message. Somehow I knew that what I dreaded the most was now my reality. My hands became damp with sweat and began to tremble. I felt it in the pit of my stomach and in my throat until I stopped breathing. The limp, lifeless page, dangled from my hand. "Leave…three weeks…authorities will come after you." What? I was no criminal. I had done everything by the book. I had lived there in Texas for three, very long years. This was no green card. It was a deportation letter.

I was a twenty-two-year old adventuress, a new graduate, moving from Canada to the United States. I was as excited as anyone could be. My goal was to get to San Diego, California, where friends and strangers alike had told me I'd fit in well. It was the 1980's and job opportunities for a Registered Nurse were plentiful. I was a risk taker; I just didn't know it back then. I was exhilarated as I moved away from my parents and my first love boyfriend of five years to start a new life, in a warmer country, filled with exciting new adventures.

That deportation order was the first significant adult life challenge I had to overcome. It was a serious threat to my dream. The H1 Visa that allowed me to work in the United States had expired while I was awaiting my green card, making me an illegal alien. If I quit working, my necessary sponsorship in this country would be lost. I was stuck in a seemingly unfair "Catch 22" situation. Why did the immigration department give me only 'three week's notice?' Four weeks notice was required for both my job and my landlord. Not only that, but it was nearly Christmas and I had formed a serious relationship with a man and his four-year-old son. Yet, I had no choice, I was being deported.

During the trip back to my native country, I found ample time to reflect upon my situation. I knew the "system" had serious flaws, but what could I do about it? Things were out of my control. My dream of sunny skies and sandy California beaches was fading fast. I was filled with anger and fear. I had a giant barrier in my way, namely the government of the United States. I felt totally alone against it.

Back in Canada I found that time had a way of easing my frustration about the forced change and I realized that it could have purpose for the greater good. At home in the "Great White North," I was able to spend an additional year with my family and friends. I gained insight into my love relationship and decided it was time to move on. After I analyzed my experiences, I had a greater determination and new sense of power. I finally received my priceless green card.

Each day I was getting closer to my dream of California and adventure. My dream finally was beginning to materialize and I remember every detail. My plain black van was weighted down with all my worldly possessions. My coveted red Corvette was in tow. Hours passed at the border while I waited within the cold concrete walls of the immigration department. The smell of old cigarettes and body odor lingered in the stale air. I thought I heard my name, but dismissed it. Then a loud, authoritative voice called out again. An intimidating uniformed officer summoned me into a small interrogation room. The man, planted behind his worn, heavy desk, prepared to determine my fate. He asked me a battery of grueling questions. I was nervous and my responses sounded scripted. My thoughts began to drift. Were they going to probe through all my possessions and expose my innermost secrets? What if they didn't allow me into the country where I wanted to live for the rest of my life? If I were granted resident status, would I be forced to return to dry, arid Texas?

A loud voice broke into my nervous thoughts. "Miss! What is your address in the United States?" The butterflies in my stomach began to swirl. My interrogator insisted that I need a U.S. address. He did not understand my plan to get an apartment and a job upon arrival. He said that he really needed an address. The silence was deafening. I did not have an address to give. What was I going to say? I didn't want to tell a lie and say that I was returning to work in Amarillo.

Then, for a split second, I noticed a softer, sort of pleading expression come over the man's face. Was he trying to tell me something? What was he trying to say?

I gave him my former roommate's address in Texas. He saw my expression when I told him of the possible permanent residence there. It seemed that he sensed my struggle, my journey, my perseverance, and possibly my innocence as he pronounced, "You are free to go."

Mixed emotions somewhere between crying and laughing welled up inside, but I left as quickly and quietly as possible. However, as soon as my voice was no longer audible from the border, I screamed, hooted, hollered, and cheered, exclaiming to the universe that finally, finally I did it! My dream had come true after four long years. I was permanently moving to California. Tears ran down my grinning face, as my van seemed to float further and further away from the Canadian border.

Everything happens for a reason and often for reasons we do not yet understand. It took many years for me to realize that my life experiences contributed to building my character. Initially, I didn't know I needed any character-building. But this was not about my personality. It was about becoming an improved person through hope, strength, perseverance, and most important, faith. These are all qualities I would need for the rest of my life.

Audessa Siccardi

The Power of Helping Others

Mario Turchetta

THE POWER OF HELPING OTHERS...

Being generous is not a part time thing. Either you are generous or you aren't. You can give freely, or give when you want something in return. You either love to give or resent it. Perhaps you sometimes give out of feelings of guilt or remorse, when you know you're being watched. Maybe you give only when you absolutely must.

What if you could give all the time, for no apparent reason, just because you felt like it? A generous person is:

G iving
E mpathetic
N ice
E nthusiastic
R espectful
O pen
U nderstanding
S pecial

Why is it important to help others? One reason is the feeling you get when you make a contribution to the life of another. It can provide you with a sense of self-worth. Your self-esteem will grow because you have tangible proof that someone else's life has been enhanced.

Another reason to help others is that any contribution to the universe results in "abundance credits." Abundance credits are the return on giving. You've probably heard many times that what you give will be returned to you tenfold. Tithing is based on that principle; we are supposed to give back at least 10 percent. Farmers often leave 10 percent of their crop in the fields to nourish the next season's crop. This is a way to keep the soil from being depleted of nutrients. Abundant crops require a measure of tithing or giving back. So, too, do abundant lives.

Many people think mostly of themselves. They spend their lives worrying about what they can get, looking out for "Number One!" They focus most of their energy on themselves and stay entrenched in a worry cycle: "What's gonna happen to me? What's gonna happen to my family, my money, my savings, my security, and my health? If I do this or that, what's in it for me?" They are tuned in to station WIIFM; What's In It For Me?

Why not tune-in to station WIIFT? "What's In It For Them." Concentrate on the needs of others. If you do this, you will begin to focus outside yourself. Your only desire will be the welfare of others. Your life will in turn, be blessed with the desires of your heart. When you shift focus from WIIFM to WIIFT, your life will change dramatically. Your life will be more abundant than you ever could imagine.

When you encounter someone who is involved in helping others, or who seems to have a cause greater than themselves, do you find a way to be of service to them? If you help someone who is trying to help others, you will become a part of the abundance process. Try to find a way to make their mission easier. You could encourage them, or find a way to give them recognition and honor them.

The feeling you get by giving is tremendous. You somehow know that your giving will extend further than just one or two lives. Giving makes you feel involved. Find creative ways to share. It can be small things, little acts of random generosity. You could give a gift of entertainment, such as movie tickets. Whatever ways you find to give, you will have fun doing it! Make it a family activity and get everyone involved.

A few years ago, Oprah Winfrey did a show about random acts of kindness. It is a great way to help others and to teach your children to do the same. Here's an idea: When you are in the fast-food drive-thru, pay for the food for the people in the car behind you. You must do it anonymously though. Acts of kindness should be done as quietly and humbly as possible. The idea is to spread kindness.

Be creative. Use your imagination; the possibilities are limitless. Here are some ideas about giving:

Give without expecting anything in return.
Give in faith.
Give to the universe.
Give silently.
Pay it forward.
Pay for the next in line.
Give your time.

Thinking of ways to give and doing them will help you find your purpose. Giving is good for you. Giving is a very powerful way to enhance the lives of others. Start giving today! Giving is a powerful way to enhance your own self-image and self-respect.

The power to give, and to give freely, is within your grasp; you need no one's permission to use it. You have the power—right now.

Mario Turchetta

Accentuate the Positive & *Illuminate* the Negative

David M. Corbin

Have you ever wished that you had had that "elusive epiphany" a little earlier so that you could have known then what you know now? I guess we all have.

Well, as a business advisor, consultant, and entrepreneur, I wish I had known about *Illuminate the Negative* sooner! It's a simple methodology that has boosted my effectiveness in every aspect of my life.

The precipitating event for this realization came while I was watching a Disney video with my daughter Jenna. The dancing bear sang, "You've got to ac-cen-tu-ate the positive, e-lim-in-ate the negative." Great advice for my daughter and great advice for me, I lived by that credo for years. All the tapes and books I read seemed to echo the same message, often in a different form, but with similar meaning nonetheless—the positive should be accentuated and the negative should be eliminated.

Here's what I noticed: Too many people believe that the best way to eliminate the negative was to ignore it, not deal with it; sweep it under the rug. Well, I guess that might work temporarily to make us feel good, but it really does nothing except put the problem off until later. Eliminate does not mean ignore.

Then it hit me. Why are some of my client interventions so much more effective than others? Why do some insights and systems take hold and prosper for the long haul while other approaches, significant and pleasing, at first, slowly fizzle out over time?

The answer became abundantly clear. Those who had lasting results focused not only on Accentuating the Positive but also on Eliminating the Negative—by addressing the negative. And, before they eliminated it, they illuminated it. They didn't ignore it; they shone the light on it and took a hard, honest look at it. In a way, it is like dealing with a tumor; you first need to study what's causing it and feeding it, and where it's infiltrated. You don't just cut it out (eliminate it) without first studying it (illuminating it).

It seemed that the real winners were willing to do the work of addressing those "thousand-pound elephants" in the room—the negatives—while others simply and painfully ignored them.

"I didn't want to be labeled a negative person, so I just didn't bring it up," was a common excuse. Well, I have news for those well-intended people: There's nothing POSTIVE about ignoring NEGATIVE influences and allowing them to live and grow.

Peak performing people, teams, and organizations are grounded enough in their core beliefs and values to allow people to bring up the obstacles that need to be faced; regardless of whether they can solve them immediately. Just knowing about them, keeping them on the radar, and planning to deal with them as resources allows them to create a culture that will lead to personal and professional excellence. Frequently, just bringing the issues to the table is all that is needed—just as the vampire dies when facing the light of day. Solutions are often relatively simple once the negatives have been illuminated. You can do this. Better yet, you can create and foster an environment around you that does this. One that allows for, dare I say, asks for the addressing of the negatives impacting our lives.

A billion-dollar client of mine, known as perhaps the largest purveyor of pizza in the world, is a good example. The goals of the company were to increase repeat customers, create loyalty, and reduce the tendency of customers to order pizza from any restaurant that gave them a coupon. They accentuated the positive by continuing to give out their own valuable discount coupons.

When the negative was illuminated, here's what we found. Customers were in a hurry to get something for dinner by 4:30 p.m. They really didn't know what to order, but felt pressured to decide quickly so they simply took the easiest path and ordered from any coupon they could find.

After illuminating that situation, we began to see solutions. We brainstormed by asking questions. What if our order-takers were more sympathetic to customers' needs and time schedules? What if they became problem-solvers and actually gave customers suggestions? What if they treated them as though they were calling into a crisis-hotline and tried to understand their problems and urgency? How could we train our order-takers to say and do what truly would help customers and, in turn, help build lasting customer relationships?

The results from the changes made were spectacular. Sales went through the roof, and repeat sales did too. It seemed that the cus-

tomers responded very well to the 'problem-solving, crisis hotline' mentality.

First, we *Illuminated the Negative*, in this case, customer stress and uncertainty. Then we illuminated the order-taking process and found that the employees were not attuned to their potential role as problem-solvers. Finally, we acted to *Eliminate the Negative* by arming employees with good customer service skills and teaching them to be aware, sensitive, and positive about solving customer problems at hand; a process that would not have been possible if we had focused only on the positive—MORE COUPONS!

If you are not succeeding in any aspect of your business, don't be afraid to dive right in and find out why. Don't pretend that a problem doesn't exist. We can learn from problems and we can improve our leadership and people skills by facing and solving them. In doing so, we should be able to increase the bottom line as well.

If you are not achieving your desired success, there is a reason. Be an investigative reporter and dig deep for the negative. Talk to your customers, employees, vendors, and competitors; ask questions and take notes. Listen with an open mind and evaluate what you have learned. *Accentuate your Positive* and *Illuminate your Negative.*

Your workforce should be an area of your business with which you can accentuate the positive, but, if not, illuminate the negative and find out what you can do. Unhappy employees will not talk favorably about you or your business. They can deeply damage your reputation. They will not care about you if you don't care about them. Give them the proper respect, praise, and training.

Milton Hershey, the famous chocolate maker, knew the value of his employees. When he built his chocolate factory in rural Pennsylvania, he built comfortable homes for them to live in, an inexpensive transportation system to get them to and from work, schools for their children, and even a park with amusement rides and a swimming pool. He knew his dream of making chocolate would never come true without loyal and happy people to help him, and he accentuated them.

Here are three of my greatest tips for success:

Accentuate the Positive. Be excited about what you are doing right. Highlight it! Applaud it! Celebrate it!

Illuminate the Negative. Find out what you are doing that's holding you back. Magnify it! Analyze it!

Eliminate the Negative. Get rid of it, learn from it, keep your eyes open, and, by all means, stay Awake and Live the Life you Love.

David M. Corbin

The Power of Nontoxic Living

David and Linda Zielski

Increase the power within by taking charge of what's happening on the outside!

If we told you about a common household task that would save the rivers, oceans, and the rest of our environment, would you be interested in hearing about it? Some people probably would, but some wouldn't. If we told you that it would be a safe alternative that could protect you, your family, and your pets from daily exposure to potentially harmful materials, most of you would probably want to hear more. We are going to introduce you to just one aspect of nontoxic living and the powerful effect it can have on people and the environment.

Most household cleaners commonly available at local supermarkets contain toxic, caustic, and non-biodegradable ingredients that our families and our environment are exposed to everyday. In fact, some of these chemicals can be found in every organ of the human body within seconds after being exposed. You may ask, "Why don't I get sick or violently ill when I clean my house?" Some people actually do. Some may feel a burning in their throat or lungs; some may have trouble breathing or experience watery eyes. Some people may not feel anything. Over time they may feel effects in the form of allergies, autoimmune and skin disorders, asthma, or even possibly cancer. This constant exposure to low-level toxins can have a profound effect on our health.

Since 1980, in the United States, there has been an approximate 160% increase in the number of children with asthma from birth to four years of age. Among the general population, there has been a 75% increase. The Environmental Protection Agency (EPA) attributes much of the rise to the increasing amount of time people spend indoors and indoor air pollution. The EPA has estimated that people spend about 90 to 95% of their time indoors and are being exposed to chemicals from cleaning agents, paints, and formaldehyde, which can also trigger asthma attacks. Lung cancer in adults is on the rise as well. There have been studies suggesting that 6 of every 100 janitors in Washington State have lost time from their jobs because of illness linked to toxic cleaning products. Since World War II at least 75,000 new synthetic chemical compounds have been developed and released into the environment. Fewer than half of these have been tested for their potential toxicity to humans, and still fewer have been assessed for their particular toxicity to children.

These toxins can affect the health of your mind and your body. When the body retains so many of these toxins, it begins to fight itself. When it can no longer tolerate exposure to these toxic chemicals, illnesses such as lupus, diabetes, multiple sclerosis, and cancer as well as multiple chemical sensitivities develop. Our bodies have to fight these toxins every day, and because of this, its ability to fight viruses, colds, and flu is lessened. Cleaning with toxic chemicals exposes us to an environment that may be worse for us than being exposed to the germs that we are trying to kill.

The ingredients that you most want to avoid are pesticides, herbicides, fungicides, ammonias, butyl ethers, petroleum distillates, formaldehyde, hydrochloric acid, phenols, glycols, cresol, and chlorine bleach. They are very toxic and extremely hazardous to your health. They can enter your body by inhalation, ingestion, or absorption through the skin. If you wipe down your kitchen table with cleaners containing these toxic chemicals the toxins can enter your body not only when you breathe them, but also when your hands touch the table as you sit to eat. If you use a chemical-based dishwashing detergent, the food on your plate may be contaminated. These dangers of exposure hold true for your entire family. If exposure to these toxic chemicals were to happen only once, it probably wouldn't be all that bad, especially for adults. But we are all exposed, day after day, and children, having lower body weights, are affected even more. A baby crawling across a floor you just "cleaned" and putting his hands into his mouth, or your family pet lying on the "freshly cleaned" floor are typical examples of exposure. Wouldn't it be wonderful if they could do those things without being exposed or absorbing toxic chemical residues?

You now may be inclined to go to your cupboards and take out your cleaning products to look at the ingredients. You will most likely find that many of the products do not list ingredients on the labels. This may seem unbelievable. Is it possible that there are products in our homes that do not fully disclose their ingredients, especially those products with questionable or dangerous ingredients?

Three years ago, we found an all-natural nontoxic cleaning products company on the Internet that fully disclosed their all-natural ingredients, ingredients that were plant-vegetable and mineral-based. We ordered the cleaning products and have been so impressed with how well they work that we have never gone back to chemical cleaners! Allergies and asthma have all but disappeared. We rarely get sick, and our energy levels are up. We believe it is because our immune systems can now fight off everyday ailments. In fact, we felt so strongly about getting the toxic chemicals out of our lives that we purchased the company that manufactures these all-natural products. Now we work in a nontoxic environment as well. We have the power within to make huge changes on the outside, to make our dreams and those of other's come true. We educate people about the dangers of toxins and neurotoxins and advocate the use of natural, nontoxic products in as many aspects of life as possible.

There are a variety of companies that produce all-natural nontoxic cleaning products that are safe and effective. They fully disclose the ingredients in their productions. The people who run these companies want to make a difference in people's lives.

Our goal in writing this article is to encourage some of you to take note of the ways toxins can affect you, your family, and the environment. We want you to know that there are steps you can take to make changes. We hope that we have convinced you to switch to all-natural nontoxic cleaning products. Please be aware, that if you get rid of your old cleaners, they are most likely toxic and should be disposed of properly.

To truly experience the power within, get the toxins out of your home, your environment, and your life. A cleaner and clearer mind and body gives us more time and energy to do what matters.

ও David and Linda Zielski

Follow Your Heart

Sandy Giberson

Tears rolled down my face as I rocked myself in a fetal position. I cried in sheer anguish, hating the fact that I felt I had to leave behind my family, my friends, and my secure job. I was terrified to be unemployed and of abandoning the goals I had been so diligently working on. In two days I would be on a plane heading for Spain; alone and without definite plans. As I rocked, I asked myself repeatedly, “Why do I have to go?” Then, as a reminder, those familiar images appeared in my head.

Blazing out into the workforce at the age of seventeen, I began working and saving for my retirement. If I had planned everything right, if I worked six or seven days a week, if the stock market didn't crash and no natural disasters happened, I could be a millionaire by the age of 55—or was it 65? I don't really remember now, but know that I was working hard for that goal.

A few years before, a young girl named Molly, just out of high school, came into the hospital where I worked. As I performed her exam, she explained that she was leaving the next week to study abroad. I felt as if something was stuck in my throat. I heard myself tell her how I regretted never doing that myself. Suddenly I felt like a ninety-year-old woman, looking back on my life, looking at all the dreams and desires that I had left undone. I moved my painfully gnarled aged hands around to my arthritic back and knew that fulfilling those dreams would now be impossible. I slide back into the present and I glanced down at my able hands as I finished Molly's exam. I smiled and thanked her with a big hug. That moment had changed my life.

I realized then, that I had not been really following my heart. Since childhood, I had wanted to learn Spanish and volunteer in a third-world country. I had an image of being among poor people who wore brightly colored clothes. Somewhere between then and age seventeen, I had put my dreams aside and replaced them with goals. I let fear consume what had been in my heart. I was afraid to leave those I loved behind. I was afraid of leaving this life of luxury behind for a cruel and real world. I was afraid that I would be so moved that

I could never come back to life as I knew it. How could I leave my family and friends? Would I be able to help? I was "just me."

As years had gone by, I always felt a twinge deep in my core. I knew that all I had was a gift and that my discards could save lives. I felt unsettled with images of naked, emaciated families ingrained in my mind. Those photographs of sunken eyes told of burdened lives. They seemed to be calling to me personally. When I would see the trails of dried tears on their cheeks, I would think how ridiculous it was that I had the life I did. I wondered how it would be if the tables were turned. What if it were my skin and bones on the cover of a magazine that people pored over? What if I were hungry and overworked, with little hope for change? What would I be thinking as my sunken eyes watched as a hearty journalist snapped a photo of me? Would I be thinking about food, maybe?

After that little chat with Molly, I realized that the scarier choice would be to look back on my life and to have not done what was in my heart. I would feel that I had wasted my life by not paying attention to what was really important to me. My life would suddenly be at its end and I would feel such regret! I was pretending to be insignificant so I could live a simple life. I pretended that what I had to offer didn't matter, so I could live life easily. I realized that my simple and easy life was completely uninspired. I knew that what I had in my heart was there for a reason, and to live a life unchallenged was to live a selfish and undeserving life. I was being challenged to overcome my own obstacles in order to make a difference in the lives of others.

For the following two years I got my finances together and made plans to learn Spanish in Spain. When I arrived at the Plaza Catalunia in Barcelona, I was welcomed by fireworks and a beautiful full moon on a warm summer night. It seemed as though the celebration was just for me. The scene was very unfamiliar, yet it felt so comfortable. People from every walk of life walked briskly by, and heard many different languages, all with a common elevated energy. The sound of Andian flutes echoed off the thick walls of the buildings surrounding the plaza. My heart leapt as the sound struck my core. I knew then that I was doing the right thing. When I saw a group of Peruvian musicians playing on the street corner, I realized

at that moment that Peru was where I needed to volunteer. I had already seen myself among the people of Peru in their brightly colored clothing.

For the following six months, I improved my Spanish and absorbed the rich culture of Spain. I learned my way around and I enjoyed the warmth of the people there. I remember quietly asking a woman on a bus if I was headed in the right direction. The whole busload of Spaniards, whom I thought hadn't even heard me, began waving their hands passionately, pointing and loudly discussing my situation. Even though I couldn't understand the bantering back and forth of everyone on that bus, including the driver, I knew I was probably on the wrong bus. Suddenly, the bus stopped, mid-way to the next station, and I was mobbed off onto an unfamiliar street. I looked up at the faces on the bus in bewildered shock as the bus began to move away. There were no smiles, just rigid nods of affirmation. I began to smile as I realized I was getting a warm fuzzy feeling, even though I had no idea where I was.

Looking back and remembering Molly now, with volunteering in Peru in the works, I remember how frightening the thought of not living the life I had dreamed of living was. I was thankful that even as I rocked myself and cried, I felt assured within. I was facing my fears in order to live my life to its fullest potential. It's better to regret the mistakes I've made than to regret what I could have done, but didn't.

Going to Spain took every ounce of courage I had. That chance meeting with Molly, several years ago, allowed me to start following my heart. I had a very strong feeling deep within my core: a feeling that I had had since childhood. A feeling that was so incredibly powerful that I simply had no other choice but to pursue my dream. I am so thankful that I faced my fears and because of that, I am experiencing life as never before. I now have the courage to do what is in my heart and to live life inspired. Next step: Peru…

ᔓ Sandy Giberson

Are You a *Dream Maker or Decision Maker* Because Your Future Depends on It?

Steven Encarnacion

It starts with a dream.

What is your dream? Do you dream of the freedom of time to do what you want to do whenever you want to do it? Could it be a vision of financial freedom wherein you are empowered to help others and to change the world?

One of my favorite dreams is to travel wherever I want to, whenever I wish, and to travel in First Class. For you, it may be to pay off the mortgage, all of the bills, the student loan, or perhaps to do something wonderful for a parent, brother or sister. Dreams are beautiful things; sometimes we get such a great feeling as we imagine a future where our dreams come true. It is a feeling of fulfillment and worth; of accomplishment and pride.

What kind of dreams do you have? Do you ever feel that you would do anything if you could be given the vehicle to make your dreams come true?

The secret is to dream big; know why you want it and don't let anybody stop you.

So, if you already have the big dream; if you know why you want it, why it is worthwhile and worthy of your life's effort, then what's stopping you? Is someone standing in your way? Often, when we honestly ask that question, the honest answer is, "Yes, and I am the person barring the way."

Why would you be the greatest barrier to your dreams? Well, the answer is not easy, but it is simple. Would it be true to say that your circumstances are the result of the decisions that you have made? Would it be a true assessment to say that you can change your results if you were to make new decisions? If you agree with those assumptions, then you are ready for a great change in your life, because now all you have to do is make new decisions. The new decisions will have new results that will reflect your big dreams.

You have to be very careful of who you listen to when it comes to the advice that is going to change your life and guide your decisions. Remember, the only person who is going to tell you to second guess your decisions is someone who is probably very unsuccessful. "Misery loves company," and failing to succeed is very safe; you can always blame it on circumstance, the interference of others, genes, fate or the weather. It takes courage to remain faithful to your own dream, and that means that you have to be your own "cheerleader." Remind yourself of the beauty and the power of your dream, and don't let anyone shake your belief that you can do it.

Then you must make the decision; to make the commitment to act upon your dreams and make them a reality.

In the hope that it will help you make that decision, let me tell you about my vision for the children with catastrophic illnesses.

In some ways, I am living a beautiful dream. I'm a resident of the San Francisco Bay Area in California's Napa-Sonoma wine country. The world-renowned wine country is very beautiful; you get to see the vines produce the grapes and the colors in the fall are breathtaking. The majesty of the "Golden Gate Bridge" and San Francisco is less than an hour's drive away. To the east, is the beauty and recreation waiting for you at Lake Tahoe up in the Sierras.

Yet, with all the beauty of my world, I spent a lot of time in the past saying "I wish I had." It's a time that I really believed that I could get anything I wanted by wishing for it. Wishing for something without putting any time into the fulfillment of your desire leads to many problems. Stress, anxiety, depression, embarrassment, self-doubt, and fear are just a few of the results that come to "mere wishers."

How different is my life is today! The cause for this difference is not the lottery, or an inheritance. It is the simple realization that dreams can guide decisions, and decisions can change lives.

You may be asking, "How can I change my life? Well, it starts with a decision to change and is then followed by a commitment to change. Little by little, day-by-day, your life will change as you wish it to. After all, little by little is how you got to the place you are today.

People ask me, "How can a decision change a life?" I say, "Would you agree that where you are today is because of the decisions you have made in your life?" Often, they really weren't major decisions at all, but you made them. You may have said something like, "Its 6 o'clock; time to watch the football game." Now, that wasn't a big decision, but it was one of many easy decisions you made to get to where you are today. "It's 1 o'clock; time to play the video games with my friends." Again, that wasn't a big decision. "I'll start saving money when I get a raise; I need some fun in my life." Not a big decision, but one that matters, nevertheless. And it got you into the position you're in today. Perhaps there are too many bills to pay, "too much month and not enough money," a car that can't be trusted on long trips and a vacation that keeps getting postponed because other people and other things are in charge. It takes a decision to change, the commitment to change and you will create the new results that reflect your new decisions.

I remember when I decided about my future. My personal vision is to make the greatest possible impact on the children with catastrophic illnesses at a very special research center. These children have illnesses that no child should have to endure. This very special hospital is a leader in the research and treatment of the cancers that afflict these children. I can provide support through money, by assisting with support groups for the parents, and housing for the parents so that they can be with their children. I can visit these children, just to be with them, and to let them know that people really care. These children must be treated so that they have a chance to live a normal life.

This is the beginning of the story, and not the end. It's not where you have been; it's not where you are today. It's all about your future. Do you want to change the course of your future? Do you want to change your lifestyle? Make the decision to do so, and let the dream in your heart be the beacon for your future.

Steven Encarnacion

My Opinion
Lee Beard

There is a great line in the movie Rudy that focuses on the wonderful power within us all. Rudy goes to the priest to ask some questions. The priest tells him that there are two things that he knows: "There is a God, and it's not me."

There are a lot of things that I do not know or understand that I utilize in my everyday life.

I started to make a list of all of the things that I did not know but I realized that would take too long. I feel that my understanding of the power within came when I did a course on "Learning to Hear God." The course referenced a time when someone in the Bible was told to write down all that he heard from God. In the class we would sit quietly and write down what we felt that we were hearing from God. It was encouraging to hear people in the class share what they wrote because we were hearing some of the same things.

One of the practical things that happened during that time came when I was listening and writing with my son who was in high school. We would sit during our devotion time and see what God was saying to us. One day, he asked me to ask God if he should wear a t-shirt that he bought that had the name of a rock band on it. The answer was very interesting to both of us. What I got as an answer was that he could wear it because he did not buy it because of the rock band's message but that he should not wear it to church because it might be misunderstood.

Another time, my son asked me to see what God had to say about him. The word came to me that God loved him. It brightened up his day to know that God knew him and cared enough to love him. I have to say that it encourages me to know that God loves me and cares for me and looks after me.

In the Bible, we are promised the Trinity of the Father, the Son, and the Holy Spirit. We are also promised the down-payment in this life of our inheritance of the goodness and glory to come. The Holy Spirit is described as the Helper who is sent to abide with us forever. That has got to be a good thing.

So here is how I see it: We have a heavenly Father who is described as love. That means He is love and can be none other than love. We are also told that He cares more for us than we can care for ourselves or that we can care for our children. How cool is that?

So we have a Father that is love and a forever Helper in our lives. What does that mean to our everyday lives? How can we practically use the power within? For me, when I remember to do so, it allows me to look at things not from an ownership position but from a stewardship position. That means that the outcome is not in my hands; I'm just serving, managing, and overseeing the possessions of this world. It allows me in the good times to say, "Thank you Lord," and in the bad times to say, "Lord you've got a challenge."

Many years ago, I bought a car that I really wanted but which turned out to be undependable. It was not a happy situation. Some years later, I bought another car that I wanted but this time I put a Jesus license plate on the front of the car and said that it was not "my" car. It was a delight to drive. When I had a flat tire, I would say, "Lord, you have a flat tire."

The scriptures tell us to do for others what you want them to do for you. So I want to wish you peace, love, and joy every day of your life. I wish you your own sense of a power within.

ଓଃ Lee Beard

Author Index

Allen, Debbie *73*

Debbie Allen and Patricia Drain are Business Growth Experts. They have built and sold over a dozen highly successful corporations. After investing in their own wealth by attending business building events, they knew that they needed to create a wealth-building university on a much grander scale. So together they formed Maximizing Success, Inc., a wealth building event firm based in Arizona. To learn about their next amazing event, visit Website: www.MaximizingSuccess.com

Anderson, Betty *9*

I am a mother of two amazing children, both adults now. I started out my working life in the banking industry, began as a file clerk and worked my way up to Manager of Customer Services and Operations. At the same time I built a network marketing business, moved on to Director of Sales and Marketing for a modeling agency, sold Real Estate and in 1996 pursued networking as my full-time career.

PO Box 878
Valemount, BC Canada V0E2Z0
Office Phone:1-403-542-4389
Phone: 1-250-968-4387
E-mail: foreverabutterfly@yahoo.ca
Website: www.shaklee.ca/butterfly

Beard, Lee.. *119*

Lee is a former television producer and business developer. He lives in Arkansas when not traveling as the co-creator of the *Wake Up...Live the Life You Love* book series. Lee is an author featured in more than a dozen motivational and inspirational volumes. He concentrates on bringing the power of the *Wake Up* network to bear on the challenges of business development. You may contact Lee at: lee@wakeuplive.com

Benson, Shanda *27*

Shanda was very troubled as a child, she was "born again" at the age of 20 but by 40 she became suicidal due to the many years of suffering with Fibromyalgia. She encourages others by sharing the Love of God and her personal Story of Hope. She is a wife, speaker, author, Wellness Consultant and Home Business Developer. She loves purple, having fun, horses, spiritual and personal growth, overcoming challenges, living life with passion and purpose, and making a difference by helping others.

Daily Manna Int.
Medford, OR
Toll free: 1-877-492-9571
Websites: www.GetMyCD.info
www.MyStoryofHope.com
www.MyHealthyClients.info

Corbin, David M. *103*

David Corbin's ideas have benefited CEOs of billion dollar companies, the U.S. Secretary of VA, world famous speakers, authors and scores of others. Awarded B of A's Innovator of the Year by Margaret Thatcher, Tom Peters and others. David is best described as a hard core business advisor who designs and implements solutions with heart, humor and pragmatism.

Performance Technology Group
13863 Putney Road Suite 1000
Poway, CA 92064
Phone: 619- 300- 6925
Fax: 858 748 6060
E-mail: david@davidcorbin.com
Website: www.davidcorbin.com

Crowley, Sam ***51***

Sam and his beautiful wife Angela have three children; Madeline, Laura and Paige. Sam left his executive level job in corporate America to focus on being a father and husband. Sam is building a multi-million dollar home business and is also a motivational speaker in the Ohio/Indiana/Kentucky region. Sam looks to expand his motivational speaking business nationwide in 2006.

E-mail: sam@everydayissaturday.com.
Website: www.everydayissaturday.com
Cincinnati, OH

Di Lemme, John ***1***

As a young child, John Di Lemme was clinically diagnosed as a stutterer and told he would never speak fluently. Today, John has achieved great success as an international motivational speaker, accomplished author and multi-million dollar entrepreneur. John shocks millions globally by exposing the truth about how to achieve monumental life success despite the labels that society has placed on you. Through his award winning live seminiars, power-packed boot camps, training programs, live tele-classes, and weekly ezine, John Di Lemme has made success a reality for thousands worldwide. Visit www.FindYourWhy.com and discover how you can finally create monumental success in your life today and achieve all your goals, dreams and desires.

Drain, Patricia ***73***

Debbie Allen and Patricia Drain are Business Growth Experts. They have built and sold over a dozen highly successful corporations. After investing in their own wealth by attending business building events, they knew that they needed to create a wealth-building university on a much grander scale. So together they formed Maximizing Success, Inc., a wealth building event firm based in Arizona. To learn about their next amazing event, visit

Website: www.MaximizingSuccess.com

Dyer, Dr. Wayne *45*

Best-selling author and lecturer.

Wayne is the author of these best-selling books, *Power of Intention*, *Real Magic*, *Manifesting Your Destiny* and *Pulling Your Own Strings*.

Encarnacion, Steven.. *115*

Steven was born in Pittsburg, California, located in the San Francisco Bay Area. He and his wife Gail share the same passion for their country's recreation areas. They like to hike where ever there is red rock. Steven is an International Champion Recruiter. He has very big goals and visions to do more than his share to help children with catastrophic illnesses.

1204 St. Joseph Way
Petaluma, CA 94954-5360
Office phone: 1-866-575-2648
E-mail: steve@creatingactionhabits.com
Website: www.creatingactionhabits.com

Farrow, Ardice *81*

A former media designer, Ardice is the creative mind behind many imaginative and award winning products for Lucasfilm Learning, Disney and others. She has spent decades learning how to capture people's attention with imaginative stories and move them to new realms of discovery and possibility. Ardice is a bold, new voice in the world of transformational living. She is currently speaking, writing and conducting national seminars.

Phone: 415-378-2816
Website: www.ardicefarrow.com
E-mail: WakeUpArdice@ardicefarrow.com

Frances, Shelli...*31*

Shelli Frances is a single mother of two awesome daughters Kati and Cami. They reside in Southern California. After years of perfecting her craft, she eventually recorded her first demo CD in the heart of Nashville. Shelli's vocal talents have garnered a fan base as far away as Europe. Her signature song *I Will Shelter You* was the catalyst that created her non-profit foundation Kind Hearts 4 Humanity, which is currently raising funds for disaster relief. To learn more, visit www.shellifrances.org and hear a sample of *I Will Shel*ter Y*ou.*

Giberson, Sandy...*111*

Sandy is currently opening Aqua Bella Spa in Desert Hot Springs, CA. With its own source of natural mineral hot springs water, Aqua Bella Spa focuses on holistic Spa treatments. Featuring pieces from Tibet, China and India, luxurious Aqua Bella Spa maintains a sacred healing. Recycling, reusing and conserving, Aqua Bella Spa strives to nurture the client as well as the environment.

Website: www.myaquabella.com
Phone: 619-316-1986

Harris, Simon A. *69*

Simon Harris is a Christian, involved in Network Marketing with Glyconutrient company. Mannatech is the 6th fastest growing small business in the United States, bringing the gift of health, hope and prosperity; making a difference by dreaming the impossible. As an optician I also did a number of eyecare camps, testing eyes and prescribing with UK charity Vision Aid Overseas (VAO), who often use volunteers from many UK prisons to clean, repair and grade used spectacles which are then shipped out with teams of optometrists and distributed to wherever they are most needed in the world. I went as a volunteer to Zambia in 1999 where one in three of the population is HIV positive, then to Armenian prisons also in 1999 together as a joint venture with the US charity, Prisons Fellowship International (PFI). In 2000 I led a team of six to southern Albania, and then during the week of September 11, 2001, I led another team of six to south-west Ghana. Each trip lasted just over two weeks and during each trip, between 1500 and 2000 local people were seen. This tends to transform local communities; the young can see to get an education, adults can work, middle-aged workers in clerical jobs can continue to work whereas otherwise they would have to stop through having no reading spectacles, and elderly people become independent, often releasing younger family members to work and bring in an income. A wonderful privilege.

Bishop's Stortford
Herts. England UK
Phone: 044 7843 670013
E-mail: sparedoor@aol.com

Hinrichsen, Mary Gale *13*

Mary Gale is married with two sons and two daughters. She authored *The Love Doctor Talks Trash*. Her PhD is in Christian Counseling. She has helped many families learn healthy communication and enabled them to trash what holds them back and recycle to get what they want.

San Diego, CA.
E-mail: mghinrichsen@cox.net
Website: www.loveisministries.com

Hudson, Kathleen *41*

Kathleen is a wife, mother, author, speaker and entrepreneur. She is the author of the forthcoming book, *The Final Companion*. Kathleen is the Executive Director of the www.Homes4Heroes.org Business Alliance and Marketing Manager for the www.BruceKingTeam.com mortgage planners. She is the CEO of His Service Inc., in Peoria, AZ.

Phone: 480-346-3350 ext 148
Toll free: 877-7-INCOME
Cell: 602-430-0891
Fax: 623-321-8032
E-mail: kathleenhudson@cox.net
Websites: www.1-877-7-income.com
www.endidtheft.com

Johnston, Beverley *61*

In her pursuit of health, prosperity and making a difference in people's lives, Beverley continues to take her athletic adventures and her entrepreneurial business vehicle throughout her home province of British Columbia and worldwide.

Network Marketing
Vancouver, Canada
Phone: 604-872-4791
E-mail: beverleyjohnston@telus.net

***King, Barney*..........21**

Barney is a dynamic and visionary executive with 20 years of experience as a senior manager and CEO, developing empowered, self-motivated, results-producing teams. Macnas Consulting solves a broad range of organizational, product development and operational challenges. Barney is an outstanding speaker and seminar leader.

Please contact him at:
Macnas Consulting International, Inc.
4980 Beauchamp Ct.
San Diego, CA 92130
Phone: 619-417-5582
E-mail: barneyking@macnas.us
Website: www.macnas.us

***King, Bruce M.*..........65**

Bruce is a husband, dad, grandfather, author, speaker, and business leader. He is also a retired U.S. Army Major, who was able to successfully transition from twenty years of public service to the business sector. Currently he is one of the leading mortgage loan officers in the country and enjoys mentoring people in the business. Bruce is passionate about serving others and about helping people realize their potential.

3126 E. Gary Street
Mesa, Arizona 85213
Phone: 480.329.4478 Fax: 480.664.8956
Website: www.brucekingteam.com
E-mail: brucemking@cox.net

Kunau, Kathy A. *5*

Kathy, a former real estate executive, is living the life she loves helping others experience the extraordinary life she believes God intends for all. As a Life Consultant and author, utilizing her fourteen years of research and experience in life enhancement methods, Kathy employs the latest in technologies to help others identify and transform what is blocking them from living the life they love. Kathy's passion is rapidly catapulting her clients' lives beyond the ordinary to the extraordinary.

Website: www.kathykunau.com

Motter, Robbie *91*

Robbie Motter wears many hats. To name a few, she is a Master Certified National Speaker, Certified Business Coach, DIVA, writer and a radio and television talk show co-host. She is also the Western and Regional coordinator for the National Association for Female Executives.

27701 Murrieta Rd. #30
Sun City, CA 92586
Phone: 1-888-244-4420
Fax: 1-951-679-8148
E-mail: rmotter@aol.com
Websites: www.rmotter.com
www.diva-registry.com

Reid, Gregory Scott *59*

The #1 best-selling author, Gregory Scott Reid has become known for his energy and candor on the speaker's platform and his signature phrase, "Always Good!" An experienced entrepreneur in his own right, he has become known as an effective leader, coach and "The Millionaire Mentor."

Phone: 877-303-3304
Website: www.AlwaysGood.com

Rogers, Stephen D. *3*

Stephen is an author, teacher, speaker, hiker and healer. As the visionary founder of Shen Life, he teaches others how to integrate their humanity into their spirituality.

Shen Life
3601 Ocean View Blvd. Unit H
Glendale, CA 91208
Phone: 818-249-9141
Phone: 866-497-SHEN
Website: www.shen-life.com

Rousseau, Stacey A. *47*

Stacey is the proud mother of two children, a co-author, reiki practitioner and entrepreneur. She focuses on creating wealth and residual income for herself and others, as well as embracing and flourishing peoples' inner creativity, desires and happiness. It is her energy and outlook on life that attracts people to her and her businesses.

325 West Shore Rd
Alburg, VT 05440
To learn more about Stacey, please call: 802-309-1222.
E-mail: stacey_rousseau@yahoo.com

Sampson, Jasmine *55*

Jasmine lives with her husband Robert Jenkinson between England and her native New Zealand. Through her international business, Freedom on Purpose, Jasmine is achieving her personal goal of empowering 100,000 people worldwide to identify and develop their personal gifts, live the Divine Dream that is in them and fulfill their Unique Purpose in life.

Phone: +447765562610
E-mail: lifetransformations@gmail.com

Shotts, Dewitt ***39***

Dewitt Shotts is the president and founder of Marketing Solutions Inc. in Little Rock, AR. With more than 20 years experience in the proprietary school industry and almost thirty years experience in direct response, Dewitt primarily directs the creative side of Marketing Solutions. In 1987, Marketing Solutions began as a television media buying service, but has expanded into a full service company with television studios, a full service direct mail and print facility, and the most recent addition, our website that includes educational and general directories. Dewitt is a frequent speaker at state and national conventions.

1601 Westpark Dr Ste 103
Little Rock, AR 72204
Phone: 501-663-3433
Fax: 501-801-5100
E-mail: dewitt @msileads.com/about/
Website: www.msileads.com

Siccardi, Audessa ***95***

"The Complete Image Consultant"

Audessa Siccardi is a unique talent with a decade of experience helping others to reach their optimal physical and inner potential. As a professional teaching skin care and makeup artistry, her creative interior design background and color expertise sets her apart from the ordinary. Audessa shares her wisdom teaching worldwide tele-classes so women and men can discover the possibilities for their new and improved, complete image. Audessa resides with her husband Dave and son Jordan in Carlsbad, California and is available for speaking engagements including topics on health, beauty, image and self- improvement. Author of: *99 Treasures to Embrace*.

E-mail: info@thecompleteimageconsultant.com
Websites: www.thecompleteimageconsultant.com
www.marykay.com/asiccardi
www.UniversityofMasters.com/audessa.html

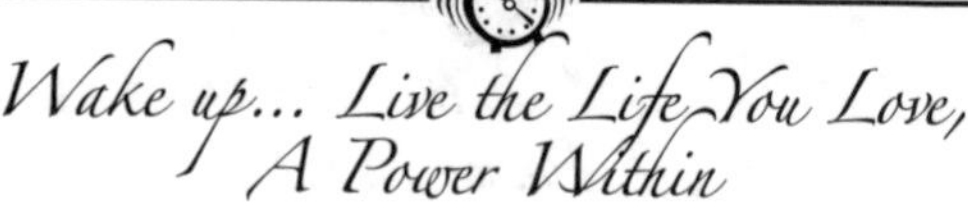

Stavroulakis, Erofili *87*

Erofili is an entrepreneur, co-author and serves as Holistic project developer for cancer. She is also involved in prosperity teachings and philanthropic projects for the community. She has been in practice as a mind-body therapist in natural therapies with a focus in counseling, as well as Bowen Therapy, since the turn of the new century. Erofili is on track to living the life she loves. Discover how you too can join the motion.

Phone/Australia: 1300 558 430
Phone/International: +61 (0) 419 626 828
E-mail: erofili@jointhemotion.com
Website: www.jointhemotion.com

Steven E. *19*

Creator of the number one best-selling series, *Wake Up...Live the Life You Love®*.

E-mail: stevene@wakeuplive.com

Turchetta, Mario *99*

Mario is a trainer and author who helps others reach their goals through coaching, training and team building strategies. He is the founder of THETOPTEAM, an international organization of independent leaders working together by helping others enjoy wellness and build secure financial futures with residual income.

20, 20th Avenue Terrebonne
Quebec J6Y1H9 Canada
Phone: 514-241-4068
E-mail: thetopteam@videotron.ca
Website: www.marioturchetta.com

Linda has been in Emergency Medical Services (EMS) as a volunteer First Responder or Emergency Medical Technician (EMT) since 1978. She has also trained Search and Rescue (SAR) dogs for 13 years. Her volunteer experience and entrepreneurial spirit led her to form Em Paks™. Em Paks™ specializes in educational programs for groups and companies. We also design and market Emergency Preparedness Paks for individuals, groups, and fund-raising organizations. Our Mission Statement is helping others help themselves through education.

Phone: 434-979-7257
E-mail: Linda@empaks.com
Website: www.empaks.com

Teri's quest for excellence is best expressed in her one-on-one coaching, public speaking, books and audio programs. As founder of Walking in Excellence, a consulting and mentoring program, Teri motivates others in connecting and creating a culture of excellence through her series "Desperate for Destiny." As co-founder of a home-based business, she grew the company into a publicly-traded multi-million dollar corporation. Teri is widely respected for her wit and wisdom, thereby effecting change and creating successful outcomes through incorporating spiritual principles in business and life.

Phone: 972-763-1922
Office phone: 800-434-4866
Website: www.teriwerner.com

Yeo, C. John, RNVR RTG.. 15

John, a former toolmaker, draughtsman/designer immigrated to Canada in 1966 with his first wife Kay. He was a sailing instructor in Vancouver, and worked in several companies as a draughtsman. John moved to Calgary in the late 60's and worked with a large power company as a technician. "People wonder about the RNVR RTG," he says"and I was in the Royal Navy and the Royal Navy Volunteer Reserve, but to me it means, "REVITALIZED! NOT VERY RETIRED REARING TO GO."

E-mail: cjohnyeo@authorforjoy.com
Websites: http://authorforjoy.com
http://www.mannapages.com/forjoy
http://www.cashflow724forjoy.com

Zielski, Dave... 107

Dave has more than 15 years of product design experience with technology development firms. He is a graduate of Wentworth Institute of Technology in Boston, Massachusetts and has had graduate studies in computer science at both New Haven University and Columbia University. Every year, through Linda's constant education and enlightenments, Dave has led a healthier, toxic free lifestyle.

Dave Zielski, President and COO
Seaside Naturals
PO Box 2097
Short Beach, CT 06405
Phone: 1-203-484-7777

Linda is a mom, and the founder and creator of Seaside Naturals LLC, which was started in Short Beach, CT. She is well-versed in alternative healing options and has more than 20 years of experience with a well-rounded combination of natural products and treatments. Linda holds a Bachelor of Science Degree in Exercise Physiology and Nutrition with an interest in environmental studies.

Linda Zielski, CEO
Seaside Naturals
PO Box 2097
Short Beach, CT 06405
Phone: 203-484-7777